AF884369

BIG MONEY SECRETS

"Compound interest is the eighth wonder of the world. He who understands it earns it... he who doesn't... pays it."
~Albert Einstein

BIG MONEY SECRETS

"There are people who have money and people who are rich."
~ Coco Gabrielle Chanel

Stan M. Steele, CMPS

This book is dedicated to

Charmaine
Stan III
Taji
Kedar

You are my WHY…

TABLE OF CONTENTS

CHAPTER 1

TIME FOR A NEW PLAN

"Why 97% of IRA investors need this book"

> *"The one thing stronger than all the armies in the world is an idea whose time has come" ~ Victor Hugo*

Within these pages, you will find simple steps that you can implement starting today to improve your financial future. This book will provide you with 7 Steps to financial independence.

Financial Independence – What exactly is financial independence?

It's reaching the point to where you have enough money to cover your needs and basic wants after taxes and after accounting for inflation for a specified period (usually you and your beloved's lifetime). The amount of money needed to achieve financial independence is called "Critical Capital". This is a pile of money that can sustain all retirement expenses with inflation and after taxes for a specified period of time. This may be an assortment of piles of money; Note Investments, 401K, ROTH IRA, or even taxable money. You can be financially independent and still work a job just for fun…as opposed to working because you need the money.

Even though we discuss aging, and retirement income this book and the principles, techniques and strategies contained herein are not intended to be used exclusively for retirement planning.

These are wealth-building strategies and are designed to help you increase your cash flow substantially so that you can begin living the life you desire now…while you are young enough to enjoy it. In fact, when followed as outlined, the strategies in this book are designed to yield double digit returns within one to five years. However, re-investing of profits yield far greater returns over time due to the effects of compound interest.

Once you understand the principles of how the time value of money works as it relates to discounted notes your mind will be expanded far beyond the boundaries of financial mediocrity. In this bookyou will learn:

- how to evaluate a note deal for profitability and suitability for the debtor
- how to structure high-quality, high-yielding deals to increase your income
- best-practice safety measures to protect your money
- how to turn a liability into an asset
- how to create cash flow and long-term wealth from note deals

The techniques covered in this book will fall under three basic categories:

1. Buying seller-financed notes that were created by other people
2. Private Lending- Lending money to other people to buy investment properties (Ideal for creating high- yielding short term investments)Excellent strategy for creating quick profits

within 3 to 18 months

3. Creating notes when you're buying and selling properties (great for creating notes for long term hold or to sell for a quick profit

Benefits of note investing

- Easy to learn: These note investing strategies are easy for the average person to learn and implement immediately

- Hassle-free: There's no dealing with tenants, trash, toilets or property taxes with note investing

- High Yields: Well-structured real estate notes yield consistent, double-digit returns

- Safety: Secured by real estate

- Liquidity: A real estate note can be sold quickly to access the cash in emergency situations

- Collateral: Real estate notes can be used as collateral when securing lines of credit and portfolio loans

- Cash Flow: Real estate notes provide excellent cash flow

- Rapid wealth creation: Note investing is a proven way to rapidly build wealth

If you have any type of retirement savings account at all there's a 97% chance you need to read this book. By the time you're done reading this chapter, you'll realize that it may be time you consider other options outside of traditional investment vehicles. You'll see that there's no need to waste your time studying the stock market and trying to wrap your mind around commodities, sector rotation, indexed v/s actively managed funds, ETFs, bonds, or whatever investment strategy you've been grappling with.

It perplexes me to no end how some people continue to gamble their life savings year after year no matter what the market does or how many Americans lose their shirts. The 60's R&B group, "Main Ingredient" said it best with the lyrics, "everybody plays the fool sometimes". But for millions of Americans, it's not just sometimes… it's a lifetime of playing the fool- listening to commissioned salesmen called stockbrokers and analysts. I just don't get why anyone would invest so much of their hard-earned cash into these exotic forms of investment vehicles that they have no way of controlling. People gamble their entire life savings in an emotionally driven market. They don't like to admit it but it's a gamble. Not very different from the gambling that takes place in the casinos of Las Vegas. You would probably conclude that someone had a real problem and needed help if they told you that over the last several years they'd spent five days a week in the casinos gambling their life savings, "But no," they would reply, "I play the roulette table some days, then blackjack other days, I also play the slots because the risk is lower see… I have a diversified gambling habit" Well I'm here to tell you that if you invest your life savings in the stock market 5 days a week then you have a problem as well. But don't beat yourself up about it. You've found this book so you're on the right path towards putting together a plan to take corrective action.

Active traders waste countless hours of their lives studying charts and data attempting to extract that one dataset that's going to give them a clue as to which direction the market is moving next. Trying to time the market is like trying to catch a fistful of wind. Time is precious, why spend so much of it trying to understand something you simply cannot control? I mean, look, let's be real, you can research and study the market until your eyes bleed and there's still nothing you can do to control the ex-factor known as human emotion which by the way, is manipulated by the powers that be. Nor can you negate the old proverb that sums it all up in four words, "the house always wins". That's a fact proven decisively in a study published in the February 2001 issue of *Financial Analyst Journal.* The study tested and compared the results between market timing and buy and hold strategies over a period of five years to determine which strategy was most effective. The study analyzed a variety of monthly, quarterly and annual market timing strategies which produced over one million possible market timing sequences with more than one million different outcomes, each of which was compared to the buy-and-hold strategy for the same time period. The results showed that the buy- and-hold strategy beats market timing 99.8% of the time. To give further credence to this notion I'll direct your attention to a study conducted by Terrence O'Dean, former researcher in the field of behavioral finance at the University of California at Davis. His study was published by the Journal of Finance. O'Dean studied the trading records at a large discount brokerage firm. He analyzed the accounts of 78,000 households over a six-year period from 1991 to 1996. His goal was to determine who makes more money, active traders or investors who buy and hold. O'Dean's study revealed that active traders underperformed the stock market by 10% per year. On the other hand, average households underperformed the stock market by only 1% per year. Incidentally, that 1% is equal to the fee investors typically pay to own mutual funds... The study further showed that active traders underperformed not because they picked bad stocks. Instead, it was their extensive buying and selling which created substantial trading costs and each time they sold for a profit they lost as much as 50% of those profits to federal and state income taxes.

Now you might read that and think to yourself, "that settles it, I'm gonna pick a stock and dig my heels in until it's time to cash in." That seems like a logical approach given the aforementioned data, right? Before you rush to judgment allow me to further elucidate the landscape for you.

Long term or buy-and-hold investors who follow the advice of their brokers as well as those who conduct their own research base their investment decisions on the analysts' reports issued by Wall Street firms. Every major Wall Street firm employs stock analysts. The analysts' job description, in a nutshell, is to investigate publicly traded companies and issue recommendations that influence public perception and market movement. These analysts are allowed to own the exact same stocks for which they issue reports. If the analysts tell investors to sell, they will negatively impact stock prices, which will, in turn, hurt their own investment portfolios.

Conversely, if they tell investors to buy the price rises. One of the most interestingly absurd traditions of the market is that many Wallstreet companies provide earnings guidance which analyst include in their reports. Considering the lack of ethics in the very underpinnings of the system it's no surprise that not a single one of the companies in the S&P 500 index has a majority sell rating...

And what about Initial Public Offerings (IPO's)? An investigation conducted by Institutional Investor magazine revealed that stock analysts are permitted to own stocks in companies they rate at virtually every major brokerage and that many of these companies are not yet available to the general public. By investing in pre-IPO stocks, the analysts have a vested interest in providing an endorsement of the IPO to consumers so the stock will get a huge boost in growth on the first day of public trading. So, you see, there is an inherent conflict of interest with regards to the role of the Wall Street analyst.

You may find solace in the fact that you have a financial planner on your team. Perhaps you've consulted with your planner numerous times over the years and feel comfortable deferring to him/her when it comes to all the tough decisions and planning out your financial future. I won't try to talk you out of this position. What I will do is point you to an observation made by Robert Kiyosoki in his 2006 presentation televised on PBS: Mr. Kiyosoki stated, "all planners are either salesmen or employees," of the Wallstreet banks... Do you really think that a salesman would direct you to go purchase a product outside of her/his company's offerings? Like I said earlier, "the house always wins". One of the most threatening aspects of our financial system today revolves around the pension funds relied on by teachers, law enforcement, fire fighters and government employees. For several years now most of the pension funds around the nation have been severely underfunded. So much so that in order for them to not go bust they must earn a 7.5% return on investment. In an attempt to achieve this end these pension funds at the direction of state and local politicians are investing in corporate credit. This gives corporations an almost limitless supply of free capital which they in turn use to buy back shares of their own stocks. These large-scale buybacks artificially inflate the value of the companies' stocks. This leads to a false sense of security amongst investors who are looking at these valuations as signs of a legitimate bull market. A little research will reveal that in the past decade the majority of the buying activity in equities has been via corporate stock buybacks, not individual investors. In other words, the market is grossly overvalued. Commercial real estate is heavily intertwined in this game of musical chairs as many of the credit funds are big on the current trend of investing in commercial real estate.

This has been going on for the past decade. What do think will happen when this manufactured bull market ends? How will the pension plans, 401k's and stock market in general react to the massive vacuum that results? The outcome can't be good for anyone except the CEO's and Wallstreet giants. Be on the lookout for a crash in commercial real estate. This will be one of the first major signals of the collapse of this house of cards... Millions of stock market investors have already been bitten by this two-headed snake in the last crash. Yet, so many of them stayed invested. Why? Because their stockbroker told them to stick it out for the long haul and they don't know what else to do. After all, the broker has no less than 100 letters behind his name and he works for one of the biggest firms on Wall Street. A firm that lives and dies on the recommendation of the analyst... And don't look to bonds, CD's and money market accounts for shelter. According to QZ.com's economics and markets reporter, Eshe Nelsonight in her June 2019 article entitled, "$12 trillion of negative-yielding bonds are sending a clear message of distress", some 12 trillion dollars in bonds are paying negative interest rates. So obviously bonds are no haven. How would you respond if you gave your aunt your money for safe keeping but when you came back a few days later to retrieve it she told you that she didn't quite have it all? Would you continue to let auntie hang on to your money? As I stated earlier, if you have any type of retirement account at all there's a 97% chance that you need to read this book. I say this because there are 27 trillion dollars invested in IRA's and of that number only 3% are self-directed. How long will you continue to allow your hard-earned dollar and the future of your family to be manipulated by the hand behind the curtain?

Right now in 2019 most of the smart money in retirement accounts is self-directed. Given everything you've just read, it's no wonder why. Unfortunately, only about 4% of the 30 trillion dollars invested in the market are in alternative investments such real estate notes etc. This is potentially tragic when you look at the financial status of most Americans. Here's what I mean:

- 75% of workers age 55-64 have less than 50k set aside for retirement.

  How are those people going to survive beyond their peak earning years? Several states are dealing with hundreds of millions in unfunded pension plans

  Bonds have traditionally been considered a safe haven for investors but that's no longer the case.

- California, Kentucky, Illiois, New Jersey and Hawaii come to mind immediately. Wallstreet is responsible for this fiscal death spin.

  When you look at the expenditure gaps in pensions, infrastructure, school funding as well as an ever-increasing budget deficit it's clear to see that you can't depend on Wallstreet to protect your pension plan

If you were a passenger asleep in your own car and you suddenly woke up and realized that the driver was inebriated you would no doubt find a way to seize control of the vehicle before something really bad happened. Well for many investors, this is your wakeup call. The driver (Wallstreet) is pissy drunk and you need to do something before it's too late. And this applies to baby boomers more so than anyone else. I say this because for the next 10 years or so, 10,000 Americans will be turning 65 each day. Do the math on that and then take a guess at how many of them are ill-prepared for retirement. For many of them, their biggest fear is outliving their money. This is a valid concern considering the average person in America lives 18 years past retirement. Most don't have anywhere near 18 years' worth of savings. This is a potential crisis of epic proportions. These people need help. And most of them have no idea that the money sitting in there retirement accounts can be used to save them from impending financial doom. They are confused and uninformed about their options. The people they have depended on to manage and direct their investments have led them astray and by the time many of them realize it, it will be too late. If they understood how easy it is to roll their money over into a self-directed IRA and invest in high-yielding seller-financed notes they could eliminate the fear of outliving their money. They could get a lot more enjoyment out of their golden years and still leave a nice inheritance for their children's children. I wish that I could have a one on one conversation with them all but that's not possible. Perhaps a few of them will gain access to the information in this book and be spared the agony of living out their golden years in poverty. As you read the chapters ahead, you will no doubt see that there is no embellishment in these words. Aside from the names of the characters and cities in the stories to follow, I give you nothing but facts and figures. If they flesh out, you have nothing to do but make a choice between the path to prosperity or that of mediocrity…or something worse.

I'd like to take a few moments to talk about real estate investing. It's no secret that real estate has created more millionaires than any other business since the founding of America. There's no shortage of television shows reinforcing the image of the wealthy guy or girl cruising the streets in their luxury car buying houses like monopoly pieces. It's so sexy, isn't it? Who wouldn't want to earn a living houses? It's easy. You just find an old dilapidated house, convince the owner to give it to you for pennies on the dollar, knock down a few walls, update all the mechanicals, install shiplap feature wall, add some sod and flowers for curb appeal and list it for twice what you paid for it. Sounds too easy right? That's because it is.

I love real estate investing. In addition to my portfolio of notes, I own or control a variety of properties ranging from mobile homes to large tracts of vacant land and apartment buildings. While it is possible to build a tremendous amount of wealth investing in real estate, what must be understood is that you need to have some disposable cash, the aptitude to learn a system and the work ethic to wash rinse repeat the system each and every day. What most people don't realize is that the sexy, picture-perfect Hollywood version of house flipping is not an accurate depiction of what it's really like for most flippers operating in the trenches on a day to day basis. The truth of the matter is that in the real world most new real estate investors have a rough time making ends meet. It's kind of a feast or famine lifestyle.

Most newbie investors are sucked into a get rich quick advertisement offered by some guru on You Tube who's perched on the hood of a Lamborghini parked in front of a mansion. After paying a nominal fee for the introductory course they end up getting baited into a much more expensive training that all but guarantees to make the new apprentice the next real estate rags to riches superstar. Unfortunately for most it just doesn't work out that way. Most are met with the cold hard reality of just how unprepared they are to deal with all the moving parts.

There are a host of challenges that often prove to be too much. One major challenge is the learning curve and the level of commitment required to be successful in the business. There's a plethora of reasons why it just doesn't work out so well for most who venture into the dangerous, shark-infested waters of real estate investing. I've seen countless would-be investors lose it all drowning in a sea of debt because they underestimated repair costs, or their contractor ran off with all the money and material. Or maybe they managed to successfully renovate a few properties only to become overburdened with maintenance issues created by tenants misusing the properties and or not paying rent. They end up house rich and money poor with enough liability to wipe out many years ofhard- earned savings. This is just a small sampling of the most common issues that newbie real estate investors face. As you can see, the list of things that can and do go wrong in the real world of real estate investing can go on and on… However, just like in any other business there is a right and a bass ackwards way to do things when investing in real estate. Unfortunately, you can't learn them all in one sitting. You can't learn them all in one year even. For this reason, I always recommend that those new to real estate investing learn to profit off of deals with as little money out of pocket as possible if they don't have a mentor. The worst thing you can do is jump in head first paying cash for houses without a mentor. In other words, if you're gonna pay for a lesson try and get the lesson in the classroom, not the closing table or the courthouse steps… And beware of mentors! All mentors aren't created equal. I've heard stories of fast-talking guys holding themselves out as gurus driving people around rundown neighborhoods tricking them into overpaying for houses, offering no guidance or support after the closing, essentially setting them up to fail. I think the words coach and mentor are thrown about just a little too willy nilly nowadays. As someone who's been a coach in wrestling and other forms of martial arts. Not to mention being trained by some of the best coaches in the world over the years. I have a totally different perspective on the word "coach". If you want to sell products but you know you're not gonna be there to coach don't advertise coaching along with your program. Just say, "buy my stuff, it can help you make money." Don't tell your students you're goingto be there to coach them every step of the way if you know your schedule won't permit you to do so. On the other hand, there are some very good and respectable men and women in the industry teaching the right way but if you don't know anything you won't know the guys offering quality content and systems from the opportunists.

If it seems like I'm attempting to paint a scary picture of real estate investing, it's because I am. It ought to scare the heck out of you if you're new to it. I've seen too many otherwise intelligent people watch their dreams go spiraling down the drain because they invested too much of their own money in a deal that they thought would make them a handsome profit after following all the steps in some real estate investment training course. They thought they would flip a few houses and get rich overnight. Unfortunately, for most, it doesn't work out that way. As a rehabber you can make some extremely nice profits, but you don't want to try and build a business purely on that. Even if you're a licensed general contractor with years of construction experience under your belt this can be a tough business due to market cycles alone if fix n flip is your only strategy for investing in real estate. At some point, you want to address the issue of cash flow and long-term investment goals. If you decide that you want to give land-lording a try good luck! Toilets, tenants and trash have been known to drive many men and women to bankruptcy. There is a correct way to manage rental properties so that the headaches are minimized but what most people find is that it's just not for everyone.

The biggest barrier to entry that I've seen for those attempting to invest in real estate is a lack of marketing budget. Too many newbie real estate investors think that a stack of business cards and a magnet sign on the side of your truck constitutes a good solid marketing plan. Most don't know the difference between marketing, promotions and advertising. I have sat in real estate workshops and listened to so-called marketing experts encourage students to hand-write 500 post cards or letters each month, send them to the same list three times and start over with a fresh list of 500 every other month thereafter. That's a joke! Good luck with that… I could spend a lot of time on this subject but I won't. What I will say is you need to establish a budget for marketing and your budget needs to allow for a lot more than 50 to 500 postcards. I'm not saying that you can't make money with such a small campaign. What I am saying is, based on average response and pull through ratios your chances are slim and you can't build a business that way. You're going have to increase your mail volume if you want to build a business investing in real estate. If that's all you have to work with for now, you should temper your expectations and you'd better be willing to put every penny you make (if any) back into marketing until you can get to a point to where you have a descent marketing budget to work with. Just like most other businesses, you can directly correlate the success and profitability of your business by how much you invest into marketing. Whether it's direct mail, ppc, cold calling, or a mix of several strategies. Either way, you need to have money to fuel your marketing. I suggest studying marketing so that you can come to value it as the vitally important aspect of your business that it is. Too many new real estate investors and small business owners view marketing as an expense. I see it as an investment… I've seen very professionally done marketing material advertising a carwash. If the owner of a carwash who has a $20 customer spend average can invest money to advertise what makes you think that you as a real estate investor, who stands to make 10, 20 50k+ per deal shouldn't invest in marketing? I know that there are people out there promoting free marketing but if your goal is to build a business solely on free advertising via the internet and social media you've got it all wrong. If you're wholesaling, you'd better find out who the heavy hitters are in your market. I'm talking about the investors who are buying 10, 20 properties a month or more. Meet with their acquisitions person if possible and find out their buying parameters so that you can feed them deals on a regular basis. You may have to work through their realtor if they have one on their acquisitions team. These are the private equities and REITS and privately held companies that are buying up all the inventory right now. Many of them are privately held subsidiaries of offshore companies. We sell almost every single one of our non-retail deals this way. I like disposing of properties to these types of entities because they typically offer 95 to 100% of asking price via a signed purchase agreement, proof of funds letter from their bank, with $5,000 non-refundable earnest money before they even physically inspect our properties. We never have to worry about back and forth negotiations, their ability to close or any of that stuff. It's like a wholesale transaction with retail pricing. Can you run a profitable wholesale business just selling to individual investors? Yes, but in order to scale you need to establish relationships with the big boys. There are several ways to build a business investing in real estate. Sometimes it just makes sense to take on a rehab project. But I wouldn't suggest building your entire business around rehabbing. Good fix n flip deals make up about 5% of the properties on the market…if that. By the time you're done with this book, you'll realize that there is a better way…

There are two basic ways of building wealth through real estate investing:

1. Income/cash flow

2. appreciation in value.

While it is possible to benefit from appreciation in value investing in real estate notes, In this book we will focus primarily on income and cash flow.

I want to shift the focus away from investments for a moment to discuss retirement planning. I think it's a bit shortsighted to make lofty plans for turning huge profits investing without having a plan for how you want to live beyond your peak earning years. This may not be the most exciting topic. I realize that no-one wants to think about aging and retirement. I promise you that it's well worth your time to spend a few moments planning for how you want to live in your later years. Otherwise, you may just that you're stuck with the plan that uncle sam has for you and I assure you, that plan is not one to look forward to. Many Americans who live to see old age will be stuck living out their elder years in misery depending on uncle sam to be there for them. Stealing food from their cat to survive. I say this because they have little to no retirement savings. According to a report released In October 2017 by the Government Accountability Office(GAO). The GAO's analysis found that the median retirement savings for Americans between age 55 and 64 was $107,000. That's a very sobering glimpse into the future of our country. The average American lives about 18 years beyond retirement. What this means is no matter how well educated they are or what their income level is most of the people you know will be living hand to mouth beginning the day after they retire… It's not because they don't make enough. It's because they started planning for retirement too late, saved too little and invested even less. You cannot save your way to financial independence. If you're not investing, taxes and inflation alone are enough to derail your financial plan over the course of your lifetime. If you doubt that, you'd better sit down with an estate planning attorney and do the math. You can't save your way to wealth and you can't expect to invest your spare change in some random investment vehicle and somehow become wealthy due to a sudden stroke of luck. If you don't have adequate funds available to support your living expenses, lifestyle, medical expenses, etc you could find yourself living in deplorable conditions. You might have to move to a low income, crime-ridden neighborhood. You may have to regularly include cat food in the grocery list each week, even though you don't have a cat… What about travel? How will you get around? Will you be able to afford transportation? All the things you take for granted today could be suddenly unaffordable the day after you retire. In order to achieve wealth, you need a plan. The first thing you want to do when it comes to planning for retirement is figuring out what kind of lifestyle you want to live in your golden years? Do you want to own a boat and sail the east coast? Or maybe buy an RV and travel the countryside? Or perhaps you'd prefer a cozy beach house in the Caribbean during the winter months and live the rest of the year between your condo in Miami and your home in California so you can be close to your grandkids. Whatever your desired lifestyle, you want to have a plan of how you're going to generate the capital to make it all real. It's doable if you start evaluating your financial situation early enough, assess your critical capital needs and pick the right investment vehicles. The problem for most people who think it may be a good idea to start investing is they don't know how much to invest because they have no clue as to how much money they will need when they retire. Here's a quick formula to get you started on your path:

How do you calculate critical capital?

#1	How much income do you want (future dollars)?	$40,000
#2	What is your expected rate of return?	6%
#3	What is the expected rate of inflation?	2%

Formula: **#1 / (#2 - #3) = $________________**

The example above illustrates how to calculate critical capital.

Now let's look at some examples of how the calculation works in real life.

Mary's critical capital calculation

#1	How much income do you want (future dollars)?	$65,000
#2	What is your expected rate of return?	7.5%
#3	What is the expected rate of inflation?	2%

Formula: **#1 / (#2 - #3) = $1,181,818.18**____________

It's based on Mary's desired annual retirement income of $65,000. Assuming an average inflation rate of 2% and an annual rate of return of 7.5% Mary would need $1,181,818.18 at retirement. On the other hand, Mr. Blass has the same desired annual retirement income of $65,000. As you can see based on the 9% rate of return of his investment portfolio, he would only need $928,571.42 at retirement.

Mr. Blass' Critical Capital calculation

#1	How much income do you want (future dollars)?	$65,000
#2	What is your expected rate of return?	9%
#3	What is the expected rate of inflation?	2%

Formula: **#1 / (#2 - #3) = $928,571.42**____________

You may be thinking that Mr. Blass has a much more attainable retirement goal compared to Mary's. Well, maybe not. Now that Mary knows how to use the formula to determine her critical capital needs, she may decide to switch to an investment vehicle that will give her an avg rate of return of 10%. If she did so she would only need $812,500 of critical capital at retirement.

Mary's Critical Capital calculation based on a 10% ROI

#1	How much income do you want (future dollars)?	$65,000
#2	What is your expected rate of return?	10%
#3	What is the expected rate of inflation?	2%

Formula: #1 / (#2 - #3) = $812,500.00________

As you can see from the examples above, it's all about rate of return. Rate of return is the net gain or loss on an investment over a time period, expressed as a percentage of the investment's initial cost. Gains on investments are defined as income received plus any capital gains realized on the sale of the investment.

If you play around with that formula a bit you'll soon realize how detrimental it can be to your retirement plan to have an investment vehicle with a rate of return that fluctuates from one extreme to the other. That's why I believe in solid stable investment vehicles, as opposed to one with the propensity to yield returns of 8% today and a negative 3% tomorrow. Ex: If Mr. Blass' retirement account suddenly began throwing off an ROI of 3% beginning next week it could adversely impact his retirement planning. To avoid a critical capital shortfall at retirement he might have to drastically decrease his projected annual retirement income or find some other investment vehicles to supplement the shortfall. Alternatively, he could increase his monthly retirement savings contribution and or delay his retirement. Once armed with the knowledge of where he is relative to his critical capital goal he might decide to make a number of adjustments to his retirement planning. Without knowing what your critical capital goal should be you don't have a clue of how much to invest or what's an acceptable rate of return on investment for your situation.

Everyone's idea of financial independence is different and based on each individual's desired lifestyle and needs. For one couple independence is owning a doublewide on an acre of lakefront property out in the country and having cash to purchase all the bait they could ever need for the rest of their lives. For another couple independence means being in a position to live life however they choose as they cruise the high seas on a yacht 3 months out of the year. Having a plan for how and when you want to retire is the key to meeting your retirement goals. You can almost always an investment vehicle that nets a high enough ROI, assuming you start planning and implement your plan early enough. But investing without a plan and no clue of your critical capital needs could lead to a disaster later in life. Let's assume in the examples given above that both Mary and Mr. Blass are approximately the same age and started investing at the same time. Let's also assume that the two of them intend to retire as soon as they reach the critical capital target and all other things regarding their income and expenses are equal. On the surface, you may say that Mary is on track to retire sooner than Mr. Blass. That could be true, but what if Mary loses her job to a robot? How much time will pass before she finds a new job? After she finds another job will she know where to find an investment vehicle that'll earn enough to make up the lost ground? Part of the problem is that most people's relationship with money is centered around them working for money instead of the other way around. They think the only way to earn money is to work for it. The group of people who think this way are what I consider the most at risk people society. Wealthy people understand the importance of having your money work for you. Many Americans who do own investments, do so only because it's part of their employment package and they don't even consider investing outside of that. This is another problem. Why would you treat your retirement savings differently than you do your other money? Put another way, why would someone only be willing to invest money that's inside an IRA or 401k account? What about the disposable income from your paycheck? Why squander that? A portion of that money should be working for you too as opposed to sitting in a savings account or being wasted. All of your money should be treated as slaves. It should be working for you and earning you more slaves. I don't mean not to spend any. What's the point in earning money if you're not going enjoy life? Nomatter how much money you have, if you're not enjoying life you're not wealthy. However, you need to maintain a balance in terms of how you manage your disposable income. We'll discuss this further in later chapters. But for now, just understand that the process of achieving financial independence begins with evaluating your financial situation, assessing your critical capital needs and identifying suitable investments to help you meet those needs.

In the next chapter I will introduce to you the best investment strategy known to man.

CHAPTER 2

WHAT IS NOTE INVESTING?

Turn your wounds into wisdom. ~ Oprah Winfrey

Before getting into note investing and what it's all about I'd like to tell you about my journey into the world of real estate. My career in real estate started when my wife gave me Carlton Sheets real estate course 26 years ago. After studying for a few weeks, I finally got up the nerve to start driving for dollars and putting offers on houses. Within a matter of weeks, one of my offers was accepted and I closed my first deal at 23 years old. It didn't take long for me to develop a great deal of confidence in what I was doing. I got to the point where I was buying a house every month.

But I didn't feel like a success because Chet, the loan officer I was using for my closings was stealing several thousand dollars from me at each closing. If I purchased a house for 40k Chet would charge me 8 or 9k in points and origination fees. At the time I wasn't aware that there were no regulations on how much a loan officer could charge in points and fees on an investor loan. But Chet was well aware and boy did he take advantage of my ignorance. I can remember one closing where my proceeds were supposed to be 20k but by the time Chet finished pencil whipping me I walked out of his office with only 5k. Chet was all smiles...I was disgusted. I had so many renovation projects going on at the time that I was hemorrhaging money. Each week I was paying out 20 to 60k in material and labor costs. This had been going on for months. I was running out of money and needed a small infusion of cash to keep things going. It had gotten so bad that not only had I burned through every penny that I had. My wife had been home from work sick…and caring for our infant son for several months, so the combination of medical bills, business expenses and being jerked by Chet had us in a real bind. I needed money badly, so I sold a house that I had planned on keeping for at least 3 to 5 years. But Chet ruined my plans. I took that 5 grand and made a few mortgage payments on my properties, bought groceries and headed home. When I pulled into my garage, I noticed a truck coming up the driveway behind me. It was someone from the power company. He was there to shut off our electricity. In the rush to get the deal closed and pay everybody else, I had completely forgotten about the disconnect notice that we had received a week or so earlier. I had just paid everybody and bought groceries and all I had left was the money I owed Julio, my best most reliable contractor. My light bill was $350 and I owed Julio $330. I was crushed. I couldn't believe it. After all the money I had been making, there I was, down to just a few hundred dollars and literally counting change from my ashtray. I was too embarrassed to let the utility worker see my face so I waited on him to head around the side of the house and then I scurried on inside. I walked into the living room just in time to hear the last wave air from the air conditioner swoosh through the vent above my head. Everything went silent. My heart sank. I kissed my wife told her to light a candle and I rushed out the door headed back to the city. I went to every single property that I owned and started loading up any and everything that was still in a package or that still looked relatively unused. I'm talking power tools, building materials, paint…you name it. I loaded all that I could carry on the back of my pickup truck and headed back to home depot. I returned it all for a refund. I walked out of home depot with $4,500 in my pocket. By the time I got back to my side of town, the power company was closed for the day. I went home and sat with my wife and son. She had already started cooking dinner…in the fireplace. I was shocked and impressed!

Caribbean women can be quite resourceful. I explained to her what had happened and she didn't even flinch. She just looked at me and said I believe in you baby. I had never loved her more than I did in that moment.

About five minutes later Julio knocked on the door. I opened the door and went outside to hand him his check. I told him to send all his workers over to this one particular house in east Atlanta the next day so that we could finish it quickly. I already had a buyer lined up for the house where all the resources were to be shifted. The work was finished within a week and we closed two weeks later. I netted about 50k from that deal…enough to dig myself out of the hole that I was in. Once I realized I was being overcharged I kicked ol Chet to the curb. I could've let that bad experience discourage me from wanting to continue my dream of being a real estate investor but I had never been a quitter and wasn't about to start. Instead, I set out to learn all I could about the mortgage industry. At first my goal was to just avoid getting ripped off but eventually it dawned on me that becoming a loan officer made me more effective as a real estate investor. So I enrolled in loan officer training classes at a local mortgage training school. There I learned all the basics, including how to stay on the right side of the law when originating loans. After I finished my loan officer certification classes I started looking back over some of the settlement statements from my closings with Chet and it became clear to me then that this guy was a crook. From that day on, I was determined to be a voice for change in the industry. I received far more advanced financial training from two extremely successful and wealthy mentors in the areas of mortgage finance, taxation and investing. I started speaking on a regular basis at home buying workshops and community-based events. My mission was to educate real estate investors and consumers about all the trickery that existed in the mortgage business at the time. I would speak anywhere I was invited, church functions, homebuying seminars, real estate investor events – anywhere. People started to take notice and my mortgage business began to flourish. So much so that I landed a weekend gig as a real estate talk show host on 640WGST, a fox affiliate at the time in the Atlanta market. All of a sudden, I had a platform to shout from. And that's exactly what I did… I landed quite a few wealthy clients from that platform and I learned a lot about the way wealthy people think about money. That's one of the reasons I decided to write this book.

What I learned is that most high-net-worth individuals don't have anyone with any real expertise they can trust to advise them on money. Outside of their stockbroker (for those that invest in the market) they don't have anyone to turn to. What many of them do is rely on whoever they feel most comfortable with to guide them through personal challenges, career moves or cigar choices. That person could be a childhood friend, minister, former employee turned confidant…anybody at all. Usually, the person that they look to for investment advice has zero expertise in the subject matter. This can be detrimental in the long term. So, I've found that in this area I'm able to add value to the lives of high-net worth individuals.

What I know about most Americans is they are shortsighted and easily appeased by messaging from big corporate overlords operating from behind the curtain. Your subconscious mind knows full-well what's going on. But the corporate overlords lull you into a stupor with a variety of distractions cloaked under the guise of holiday functions, sporting events and anything they can use to dominate the news cycle and impact your emotions. It's like a game of musical chairs. Except this game is rigged. Guess who's gonna be sitting on the floor when the music stops. When it's time to retire the music stops if you don't have a plan. These strategies are not just designed to help you build a retirement portfolio. These strategies can be used to help you create the life you desire today. You're holding the blueprint for your plan right now. It's up to you to implement the plan. And if not this plan, you better have "a" plan.

The other reason I wrote this book is to help ordinary people build wealth by providing a blueprint for creating high-yield investments. I'm giving you over 25 years of experienced based knowledge. Knowledge that I've gained from being in the trenches doing the work, taking advanced level classes and one on one mentoring from legendary market leaders. You are the beneficiary of high-level intellectual property gained over the course of my career as a successful real estate and note investor. I own or control a variety of asset classes from mobile homes to large tracts of undeveloped forest land and everything in between. Real estate is my profession, my vocation and my passion. I've put in the sweat equity so you can reap the rewards. This little book is packed full of secrets and strategies that you're not going pick up on YouTube.

And it's not just me tooting my own horn, I've been recognized by my peers for my expertise and accomplishments for years. Just recently, I was named "One of the Top 100 People in Real Estate for 2019" by Top 100 Real Estate Magazine. But enough about me. This book is about helping you. After all, that is my passion – helping people. You want to know what note investing is all about. That's why you purchased this book...right? Well let's get into it.

Notes is a term used in the finance industry to describe debt instruments, including mortgages, trust deeds, promissory notes, contracts for deed etc. This could be any financial instrument in which one party promises to pay another party a specified amount of money over an agreed upon period of time, usually with interest identified at the point of origination. The content in this book will be focused on notes secured by real estate. Note investing refers to the act of investing in a stream of income (mortgage payments) secured by real estate. This means that at the time that one party (the lender) loans the money to the other party (the debtor) real estate is used as collateral to protect the lender in the event of a default. The lender gets a lien on the property.

This gives the lender the right to foreclose through due process of the law in the event of a default. The term note investing is often used interchangeably with other terms such as note trading, seller- finance, owner-finance, investing in paper etc. When we speak of notes in this industry we are actually referring to a series of documents such as the promissory note & mortgage or in deed of trust states such as Texas and California it would be a note and deed of trust and other documents that accompany these two documents whenever a property is purchased with financing. However, for the sake of simplicity when you see the word note, paper or any of the other terms used to describe the same just know that we are referring to a stack of papers that gives a lender the right to collect monthly payments from the debtor (borrower/ homeowner) and gives the debtor equitable title to the property and that same property is used as collateral to protect the lender.

Note investing is a very lucrative business and has been for many years. The note industry as a whole is a 76 trillion-dollar industry. It is actually the thing at the core of our banking system without which our financial system and monetary policy would be obsolete. The banks engage in very similar practices as outlined in this book with the major difference being the volume of notes traded and the manner in which they trade. Banks deal in pools, tranches and mortgage-backed securities. Their trades are done in bulk and leveraged many times over. What I'm referring to in the pages that follow are individual loans bought and sold one at a time, involving one buyer and one seller secured by one and in some cases multiple properties.

Real estate notes are superior to other investments because they're predictable and safer than anything else you can name. In a worst-case scenario with a real estate note the debtor defaults and you get the house back. You wouldn't lose your initial investment if you follow the techniques outlined in this book. This is because even in a down market home values have never reached zero in America... But when you look at other investments, it's highly possible that you could lose it all, sometimes overnight. Not so with notes. The other thing I like is you don't have to be a Harvard trained economist to understand note investing. Sure, there are a few moving parts but, in a nutshell, the only condition that's necessary is that a family has a desire to keep a roof over their head. I think that it's a pretty safe bet that most families prefer sleeping indoors under a roof as opposed to camping out on the city streets. With most other investments you have to watch the market and know how to interpret economic reports and anything that dominates the news cycle. If I'm a school teacher or nurse do I really want to have to keep track of Core CPE, jobless claims, factory orders or how mortgage bunds are performing relative to their 30day moving average?? I think I speak for nurses, schoolteachers...and most other Americans for that matter when I say, "Heck No!" Notes are simple. Whatever you bought on the day of closing is just what you have when it's time to sell five or ten years later (if you ever desire to sell). All changes are initiated by predetermined monthly payments and governed by the amortization table and the other documents executed at closing. No surprises, no extra caveats. Then there's the peace of mind in knowing that as the lender, you are named on the home owner's insurance policy so if the house burns to the ground you get paid off first - all of your initial investment plus your profit. Now that's security. The other thing about notes that I love is you don't tie your money up for indefinite periods of time. If Woodrow buys a note today he knows exactly how long it's going to take for him to earn the projected rate of return on his investment. There are so many advantages note investing has over other investments. I'll go over many of them in the pages to come so I suggest you grab a pen and notebook because there is some life-changing stuff waiting for you.

In the next chapter, I will teach you how to become the bank. You will learn how easy it is for you to grow your investment portfolio from zero to millions using seller-financed notes.

CHAPTER 3

HOW TO BECOME THE BANK

"Almost everyone pays compound interest. The key to building wealth is to receive a lot more compound interest than you're paying." ~ Stan Steele

In this chapter, I'm going to reveal to you how you can become the bank. You'll learn how to use seller-financed notes, secured by real estate to exponentially increase your cashflow.

Just about everyone pays compound interest. Whether it's a personal loan with no collateral or a loan obtained through a financial institution. The problem is most people aren't earning any compound interest. So, there's little to no compounding effect on their earnings to offset enough of what they're paying out in loans. For most Americans, this paying of compound interest coupled with a basic lack of financial literacy becomes a poverty trap. The average American only understands earning money from the standpoint of "earned income" or "trading time for dollars". This is a major problem because for most people there are not enough dollars being earned in a 40-hour workweek based on their salary or hourly wage to earn a enough income to reach their critical capital needs.

If you learn how to create assets out of thin air and earn interest on those assets you can make this strategy a consistent part of your wealth creation plan.

Note investing is profitable whether we are in an inflationary cycle or a recession. Unlike investing in brick and mortar, note investing becomes even more profitable during down markets. On the other hand, during inflationary cycles when the real estate market is hot note investing heats up even more because of the influx of capital into the marketplace. Banks understand this dichotomy. That's why they are in the business of lending money. They utilize debt instruments as an asset to create arbitrage with real estate as the collateral. You can do the same…

You may be thinking to yourself, "it takes millions of dollars to buy or invest in mortgage notes and therefore only banks are able to benefit from this type of investment". Nothing could be further from the truth. Sure, banks do have hundreds of millions of dollars. However, those dollars don't belong to the banks. That money belongs to average Americans like you and me. The banks take money thatwe deposit into our accounts and pay us anywhere from zero to around 1% interest on the money and then they turn around and lend it to consumers at 15% interest rate or more in the form of credit card debt, auto loans, etc. They do the same thing to generate profits in real estate in the form of mortgage debt. Sure, they may lend you money to buy a home at 4 or 5% interest rate but remember that's not the banks'money. The banks will payout 1% at best to account holders who let their money sit in savings accounts in the banks. That's still a difference of 3 to 4% in arbitrage. Let's assume the average bank has 300 million dollars on hand in depository accounts. Even if they only earned a 3% spread on 300 million it's easy to see how banks are able to make trillions in arbitrage. However, we know that banks are allowed to lend out many times the amount they have on deposit as a benefit of fractional reserve banking.

You can create an arbitrage too using your own money & real estate.

Let's take a look at an example of a note deal. We'll start with a typical note transaction and build upon it to illustrate a variety of note investment strategies.

Susan spent several days contemplating her financial future and deciding what she wanted it to look like going forward. She concluded that she was a girl who maybe didn't have everything, at least by most people's standards but she had more than enough to engage in her two most cherished passions as often as she liked. What are her passions? Reading and traveling. To her, everything else in life just seems to happen in between chapters and trips down the tarmac. Susan had realized using the "critical capital" formula that she needed to drastically increase her earnings over the next 3 to 5 years in order to avoid having to steal from the cat. Her only shot she was to roll the money from her current traditional retirement plan into a self-directed plan and invest in the golf course that her aunt and cousins had invited her to partner with them on several weeks prior. The partnership offer triggered Susan to engage in an intense period of research and reflection. It also demanded that she take the time to assess her "critical capital" needs prior to making a decision on whether to move forward with the investment opportunity. Susan currently lives in a duplex that she inherited from her parents many years ago. She rents the other side to a nice couple from church. Prior to inheriting the duplex, she had managed to pay off the house in South Orange that she'd previously lived in with her ex-husband. She had tried the landlord thing and after several bad experiences with tenants from hell she's decided to fix the house up and sell it. Susan looked forward to saying goodbye to that house and all the bad memories that it conjured. She listed the house for sale at a price equal to the appraised value of $250,000. Susan's house is very well-maintained and in a desirable neighborhood but due to a sluggish real estate market, it was taking much longer to sell than her realtor had projected. Susan is just about ready to give up on selling the house. She doesn't want to rent the house again because she's tired of dealing with tenants, toilets and trash. She also doesn't like the idea of having to pay taxes on avacant house.

Bob comes along and makes an offer on the house. Bob agrees to purchase the home for $250,000. He's managed to save up $60,000 for a down payment. Bob gets bad news from the Loan officer a few days after signing the purchase agreement. Basically, the bank has denied his loan because he recently had one item on his credit report show up as delinquent. Bob is devastated because he and his family have already fallen in love with the house. When he calls Susan to explain the situation she decides that although she really wants to sell the house she doesn't need to have all the proceeds from the sale at once. She and Bob agree to adjust the terms of the sale so that Bob gives her $60,000 down payment at closing, and she will create a mortgage for the balance of $190,000 over ten years plus 10% interest. To keep the loan affordable Susan agrees to calculate the $190,000 loan over a 30 year period (this means it's amortized/calculated just like a 30-year loan) with a balloon payment due in 10 years.

Loan Amount	Loan Term	Interest Rate	Monthly Payment	Amortization
$190,000	10 years	10%	$2,510.86	10 years
$190,000	10 years w/Balloon	10%	$1,667.39	30 years

As you can see from this graphic, Susan was able to reduce Bob's monthly payment by $843.47 using a longer 30-year amortization. Had she calculated the loan on a 10-year amortization the payment would have been $2,510.86, which would have made the loan unaffordable for Bob. The longer 30-year amortization allows Susan to create a lower monthly payment that will fit well into Bob's budget. You see, the longer the term the lower the monthly payment. Conversely, the shorter the term the higher your monthly payment will be. With this loan structure, Bob's monthly payment will be $1,667.39 with a payment of $187,777.07 due on the 120th

month (10 years). This gives Bob 10 years to improve his credit and qualify for a traditional bank refinance loan to pay Susan off. At that time Bob's home will have appreciated leaving him with lots of equity and a lower interest rate.

Bob Buys Susan's House

Susan owns house free & clear	Appraised Value	- 0	$250,00
Bob buys house from Susan	Sale Price	- 0	$250,00
Bob's down payment	Down Payment	-	$60,000
Susan provide's seller-financing	Loan Amount	- 0	$190,00

Loan details: Original balance $190,000 @ 10% interest per annum, compounded monthly – monthly payments $1,667.39 with a balloon payment of $187,777.07 due in 10 years

This is a true win/win situation. It gives Susan a lump sum of cash today and rids her of the stress of being a landlord and dealing with all of the headaches that come along with that. It also helps Bob by allowing him to invest the $60,000 that he's saved to become a homeowner on terms that he can afford.

After collecting on the note for three years Susan was enjoying the additional stream of income and happy that she had decided to do it. She wanted to quit her job and partner up with some relatives to purchase a golf course. However, she did not have quite enough in her retirement savings to meet the $245,000 initial investment required to purchase the golf course. Now she was stressed because she realized after thinking about it that she wouldn't be able to access the rest of the money from the house she'd sold for another 7 years. Then Susan remembered that she'd received a letter six months ago from Axiom Note Trade offering to buy her note. Susan called up Axiom and received an offer to purchase her note. On the day that she called Axiom, she was at the three-year mark of owning the note and there was an unpaid balance of $186,488.13.

The offer from Axiom was for $151,055.28 all cash with Axiom paying the closing costs. We informed Susan that the transaction would take only three weeks to close and that the title company would wire her the funds directly into her bank account. The note purchase was completed in three weeks and Susan was ecstatic. She was able to move forward with her golf course partnership.

Let's take a closer look at the numbers from Susan's perspective:

Property Sales Price:	**$250,000**
Down Payment Received:	$60,000
Monthly Payments Received:	$60,026.04 ($1,667.39 x 36 mos)
Proceeds from selling the note:	$151,055.28
Total revenue received:	**$271,081.32 ($21,000 above her original sales price)**

Susan created an asset (the note) out of thin air and was able to turn a profit that outperformed her initial plan by $21,000. This beats the heck out of selling a property the traditional way. If Susan had sold this property the traditional way the numbers would look very similar to the illustration below.

Sales Price		**$250,000**
Down Payment:	$50,000	
Seller Closing Costs:	$2,500	
Realtor Commissions Paid:	$15,000	
Seller Contribution to Buyer costs:	$7,500	
Total Proceeds from sale:	$225,000	

As you can see from the illustrations above, Susan would have ended up with over 46k less had she sold the property the traditional way through a realtor via the MLS.

You may find it hard to believe that someone would accept a mortgage with a 10% interest rate when the banks are offering mortgage loans at 4.5-5.5%. I can assure you there are many people who would gladly accept a mortgage with a 10% interest rate. Most people think in terms of payment affordability, not interest rate when it comes to a home loan, car loan or any other type of loan. In this scenario, the monthly payment is just $150 above what Bob was paying in rent per month for his previous residence. Bob, like most renters doesn't mind paying slightly more each month to achieve the goal of homeownership. Sure, the interest rate is twice as high as the rate on the typical bank loan, but Bob can't get a bank loan.

His credit is damaged. Therefore, Bob represents a higher risk. One way of shifting the risk back to the debtor is through charging a higher interest rate. The higher interest rate reduces the amount of time it will take to pay off the loan, increases the rate of return on the investment and minimizes the potential loss in the event of a default. Another way of shifting the risk to the debtor is by charging a higher down payment than usual. This is not something you do arbitrarily without determining the impact on the debtor's financial stability. You have to look at the monthly income and expenses of the debtor to determine if they are capable of handling not only the monthly payment but also the down payment and other expenses associated with purchasing and owning a home. This is really easy to do. We offer training and support to individuals who invest with us so that they know how to quickly and accurately analyze the buying power and suitability for a potential debtor. We also provide tools that allow you to analyze and qualify a potential buyer within minutes.

In addition to verifying the suitability of the loan for each buyer, we provide a list of professional companies that specialize in credit restoration services. Prior to closing, we emphasize to the debtor the importance of following through with contacting these companies and working to improve their credit. This benefits the debtor by ensuring that they are able to refinance to a lower rate and improve their monthly cash flow in the near term. It's also a benefit to us if they follow through because it increases the probability of us getting a quicker payoff which substantially increases our ROI.

From Bob's perspective, nothing changes except for where he sends his payment each month. Instead of mailing it to Susan he mails the check to our servicing company. We use a servicing company to collect the monthly payments. The servicing company receives the payment from Bob deducts their $12 transaction fee and any escrows for taxes and insurance and wires the difference to our bank accounts.

The servicing company also handles all accounting associated with the mortgage, including sending Bob monthly mortgage statements, quarterly escrow account statements, and end of year tax statements. If Bob pays late the servicing company mails out a late notice and will even work with the attorney to handle foreclosure proceedings on our behalf in the event of a default. Anyone can hire a servicing company for just a few bucks a month to handle mortgage payments. Many banks and financial institutions utilize servicing companies as well. It's really a no-brainer to me because I got into this business to build wealth not to get bogged down with paperwork and chasing after payments.

Let's look at the numbers from Axiom's perspective to see how well we profited off the deal:

Susan Sells the Remaining Payments to Axiom

Susan has collected payments from Bob over the last 3 years
Bob owes Susan 84 payments of $1,667.39 plus a balloon payment of $172,782.24

Unpaid balance still owed to Susan	$186,488.13 (plus 10% interest)
Axiom buys the remaining payments at a discount	$151,055.28 (12.75% yield)
Axiom's profit	$35,432.85

Even though the interest rate on this note is only 10% we are receiving a 12.75% yield because we invested less than the face value of the note. Remember, the original loan amount was $190,000 with an interest rate of 10% and a monthly payment of $1,667.39. We are receiving the same $1,667.39 each month that Susan was getting but with only $151,055.28 invested. Because Axiom invested only $151,055.28 we are getting a higher rate of return or yield on our investment. Our yield is 12.75% and will increase to a much higher percentage if Bob pays the note off sooner than 7 years. The sooner Bob pays us off the more our yield/rate of return increases. Most seller-finaced notes payoff in 5 to 7 years. This is another one of the most powerful secrets of note investing. The potential for ROI while maintaining a minimum return (12.75% in this case).

It's amazing how a little bit of creativity and flexible terms can allow someone to leverage real estate in such a powerful way.

If Susan had maintained ownership of that property and decided to rent it to someone instead of selling it to Bob there is no way she would have been able to find a buyer to sell that house to and access the funds in as little as three weeks. If you've ever tried to sell a house with a tenant in place you know that it can take quite a bit longer than selling a vacant house. That's partly because there are fewer people in the market looking to purchase a property that's already occupied by a tenant. Otherwise known as a turn-key rental, houses occupied by tenants present a few more moving parts that can easily break a deal. For instance, the rent may be too low. Or perhaps the tenants have damaged the property. In some cases, the potential buyer may not be happy with the terms of the lease or the quality of the tenant that's in place. There are so many things that can stand in your way when trying to liquidate a tenant-occupied property. Even if she was able to find the buyer in a reasonable period of time she wouldn't have had enough cash left over after paying realtor commissions and all the costs associated with closing to purchase the golf course. Susan made the right choice, she decided to become the bank and it paid off well.

Susan would not have had the foresight to become the bank had she not taken the time to perform Step number 2 - "assess her critical capital needs". Because Susan took that all-important step, she was able to identify her shortcoming and take appropriate actions to provide the remedy.

As you can see from the foregoing example, there is a motivation for everyone who's a party to the transaction. The thing I love about this business is that when all parties play by the rules everybody wins. In the next chapter, I will reveal how your profits go through the roof when a loan goes dark.

CHAPTER 4

HOW TO SKYROCKET YOUR ROI WHEN A LOAN GOES DARK

"Success seems to be largely a matter of hanging on after others have let go".
-William Feather

In the previous chapter we saw how Susan created an asset out of thin air to improve her cash. Some might think that the house was the asset but, in this case, for Susan, the house was a liability. I say this because it was not a source of revenue for Susan. She was not earning money on it. In fact, she had numerous expenses associated with owning the home. There was the tax bill due every year and the cost of maintenance that had become somewhat burdensome due to tenant misuse of the property. There was also renovation costs that were necessary in order to make the home marketable so that she could market and liquidate it. The note, on the other hand, was an asset that created value instantaneously the day she created it. We saw how she was able to easily sell this asset in her time of need and turn a huge profit that ultimately changed her life. What I want you to understand is that this is not a rare isolated event that takes place once in a great while. The people and companies that make up the seller- note industry engage in transactions like this each and every day totaling hundreds of millions of dollars.

In my company, we have systems and protocols in place to evaluate and vet the property, the people and the paper. However, in spite of all that we do to ensure that our investments perform as expected over the life of the loan, from time to time things will go wrong. Our job is to make sure that we follow the proper protocols to limit the number of times that loans go dark but we just don't have the ability to control what a debtor does or if his employer will decide to shutter the doors for good. Human nature and economic cycles are just a part of life that fluctuate and impact us all in spite of our best-laid plans. When I refer to a loan as "going dark" what I mean is the loan going into default due to the debtor/payor not meeting the obligations under the terms of the loan. This could mean he's stopped making payments, that he failed to refinance prior to the loan maturity date or a number of other things based on the terms of the promissory note. In this case study we are going to explore a typical scenario of just what happens when a debtor defaults on a loan.

Byron had been faithfully making timely mortgage payments for five years. He had originally purchased the property from Axiom for $360,000. His down payment at closing was $100,000. Byron had excellent credit but could not obtain bank financing because most of his income was cash from repairing race cars at the pro-custom car shop where he worked. He wasn't involved in any illegal business ventures. He was just intimidated by the thought of having to report all that cash to the IRS and never took the time to consult with a tax professional to get his business squared away. Therefore, in the eyes of financial institutions, he was unbankable. Byron lost his job when the shop owner decided to relocate to a facility two hours away. This left Byron with no income and so he stopped making payments to preserve his savings. He called Axiom up on the day that he was terminated to inform us of the recent developments and to see if there was something we could do to accommodate him until he's able to find another job. I was very sensitive to what Byron was going through. I expressed confidence that he would soon be gainfully employed once again. However, I was very clear when I informed Byron that our policy was to start the foreclosure process immediately once a loan has reached default status. After a couple of missed payments Byron's loan had indeed reached default status and I informed him that there were only two ways to stop the foreclosure process; either Byron would have to come up with the money to bring the loan current or he could stop by the office and sign a deed-in-lieu of foreclosure. "Otherwise", I explained, "we'll have to go through with the foreclosure process". I also encouraged Byron to continue his job hunt and if he was able to find a job prior to the sale then another option would be a loan modification. The loan modification would be contingent upon Byron being able to come up with at least one month's payment in certified funds and signing the modification agreement prior to the sale date.

Byron expressed his appreciation and commitment to continue his job search. Unfortunately for Byron, he was unable to a job that could cover his mortgage payment and living expenses in time so he scheduled a meeting at our office and signed the deed-in-lieu. A deed in lieu is basically a document that a debtor signs relinquishing his interest in a property to avoid a foreclosure. Byron was disappointed in having to give up his home under such circumstances, but he was also grateful to us for agreeing to not seek a deficiency judgment against him for the balance of the loan and arrearages. I thought Byron was a nice guy and didn't like having to take this route either, but I appreciated that fact that we didn't have to go through with a foreclosure. I told Byron that if he could move out within 30 days and make sure to leave the house in broom-swept condition that we would give him a cashiers check for $1,000 to help with moving expenses. I also made it a point to let him know that once he found a new job he was welcome to come apply for financing on another house if this one was no longer available. We agreed and it was done.

Benjamin Disraeli, the British politician and novelist once wrote, "there is no education like adversity". I'm sure Benjamin would agree that this experience provided our friend Byron with the education of a lifetime. I don't like to see bad things happen to good people but such is life. I learned years ago to never write up a loan for someone that I'm not willing to foreclose on. I can remember meeting Byron and urging him to go see a CPA and get his taxes in order. I could almost see my words float into one ear and out the other like ceramic horses on an old carousel. I can assure you he wished no less than one thousand times that he'd listened to me. He had excellent credit. Had he listened to me he could've refinanced to cash out some equity to hold him over until he got things back on track.

We purchased this property from a distressed seller for $280,000 5 years ago, prior to selling to Byron. At the time the property was worth $360,000. We sold it to Byron for $360,000. He paid $100,000 down payment and we financed $260,000 at 9% interest rate amortized over 20 years. His monthly payment on the loan was $2,339.29. Byron paid like clockwork until he hit a bump in the road. We were more than happy receiving an ROI of 9% but because we ended up getting the property back early from Byron our Rate of return Skyrocketed to 85.84%

Let's look at how this situation affected our investment as a company

Axiom Sells the House to Byron

Axiom's initial investment/purchase price:		$280,000
Axiom sells the house to Byron:	Sales Price	$360,000
Byrons down payment:		$100,000
Axiom provides seller-financing:	Loan Amount	$260,000

Terms of mortgage:	Original principal balance $260,000
	9% interest per annum, compounded monthly
	Monthly payments of $2,339.29

Axiom has collected $140,357.40 from Byron over 5 years plus $100,000 down payment. Our loan proceeds from Byron totaled **$240,357.40**

Now we had the house back. After inspecting the house our disposition manager determined that it was in good condition and we immediately put the house back on the market offering seller-financing. Due to appreciation, the house was now worth over $411,000. We marketed to all the renters within a 5 mile radius of the house.

Within two weeks we had several eager candidates. After carefully evaluating each of their applications he decided to sell the property to Juan, a hard-working Mexican immigrant who owned a successful painting company. Juan, unlike Byron does pay taxes on his income. He's been in business for several years and earns an impressive amount of money. However, he pays for everything cash and has no credit so banks won't touch him. Juan has $200,000 in savings at a local bank but they won't give him a loan to purchase a house. That says a lot about the intelligence behind the banking system... We agreed to take $150,000 as a down payment from Juan and financed $261,000 at 8.25% interest rate amortized over 20 years. Since Juan seemed really committed to doing the things that we recommend to build credit we felt comfortable adding a 7-year balloon on to the terms of his loan.

Here's how that looks

Axiom Sells to Juan

Axiom sells to Juan at Fair Market Value (FMV):		$411,000
Juans Down Payment:		$150,000
Axiom provides seller-financing to Juan:	Loan Amt	$261,000

Terms of Loan: Original principal balance $261,000 – at 8.25% interest per annum, compounded monthly balloon payment of $212,390.51 due in 7 years
Monthly payments of $2,223.89.

As you can see from the illustration above, we have a whole new loan in place with Juan, our new buyer. We were able to create a new loan at a higher principal loan amount along with a nice down payment of $150,000. Now you can see that it was no exaggeration when I said the ROI would skyrocket!

Total Projected Revenue from Juan's loan	
Down payment received:	$150,000
Amount of scheduled monthly payments:	$186,806.76 ($2,223.89 x 84 months)
Amount of balloon payment due in 7 years:	$212,390.51
Total projected revenue:	**$549,197.27**

Now let's step back and look at the big picture

Big Picture	
Axiom's original purchase price (basis):	$280,000 (basis)
Byron's loan	
Axiom's total loan revenue from Byron:	$240,357.40
Remaining basis from initial investment:	$39,642.60
Juan's loan	
Total projected revenue from Juan's loan:	$549,197.27
Remaining basis from initial investment:	$39,642.60
Gross revenue from both loans:	$789,554.67
Projected ROI:	**281%**

The return on investment increased exponentially due to the original debtor going into default. This case study illustrates my point perfectly. This was a great investment for us initially. Had Byron not lost his job we were prepared to carry the loan full term because we considered him a good risk. He had excellent credit and above-average income. He had also established a perfect pay history with us on the loan.

However, his circumstances changed and it created an opportunity for us to increase our ROI many times over by selling the property to a new buyer. We haven't had to take many properties back over the years but each and every time that we have done it we've realized a substantial increase in profits.

Most people have a fear of the possibility of having to deal with defaults when they enter the note business but once they become educated they soon realize that a debtor's inability to pay can represent a very fruitful opportunity for the note investor. This is because your money is secured by the property. Part of the reason I invest in notes all over the country is because I know my investment is protected by an immovable asset. Some note investors actually pray for defaultand have a sort of fast and loose approach to writing up loans in hopes that some poor borrower might get in over their head and create a premeditated hardship resulting in a windfall of cash for the investor. We have a different business model in that we structure our loans in a way that positions people for success and provide education to real estate investors and debtors with the intent to create mutually beneficial transactions that facilitate a more healthy financial ecosystem. We are all interconnected, so it only makes sense that we lookout for the best interest of everyone that we buy and sell from. This is the best defense against a society of poverty, suffering and homelessness.

I hope I've done a good job of demonstrating to you that there's no reason to be fearful of default with this example. Your most important job in this business is writing good quality loans. If you do your job right you'll profit no matter what the debtor or the economy does.

In the next chapter, I will show you how you can start building wealth with notes today even if you have very limited investment capital.

CHAPTER 5

THE POWER OF PARTIALS

"Jumping at several small opportunities may get us there more quickly than waiting for one big one to come along". - Hugh Allen

How to make huge profits with seller-financed notes even if you have limited investment capital

For years I've had friends and strangers alike approach me asking if they could team up with me and buy notes or real estate. I usually answer that question with a series of questions. That's because I need to know a few things about the individual before I can determine if they meet the minimum requirements for me to consider doing business with them. One of the most important questions I ask is, "why do want to invest in notes or real estate?" The answer to this question gives me insight into their motivation. Understanding the "why" behind the desire helps me to identify whether they have long term goals or if they're just looking for a get rich quick scheme. If they're looking to jump three tax brackets overnight, I usually advise them to go buy a lottery ticket. In my business, we don't engage in get-rich-quick schemes. Sure, we collect large lump sum checks on many of our deals, but we plan things out and create assets that are designed to generate cash flow in addition to the lump sums we take in. We have a system of protocols that yield predictable duplicatable results and build wealth over time.

Some of our better deals don't involve any large checks at all. They are smaller, lower-end homes with loan terms that produce extremely high yielding returns. Or in some cases, properties with higher loan balances where we opt to purchase partials. Buying a partial refers to buying only a set number of payments as opposed to the entire unpaid balance. This is an excellent way to rapidly accelerate the growth of your investment portfolio. This is a great strategy for people who don't have a lot of investment capital. For instance, someone who only has 30, 40 or 50k to invest could purchase a partial and easily realize exponential returns on their initial investment.

I wouldn't recommend any form of investment at all for a person who's living hand to mouth. If you work a fulltime job and are just having a hard time making ends meet I'm not referring to you. You may be struggling financially but in your 401k or IRA you may be sitting on 50 to100k or maybe even a million dollars. If this describes your, situation keep reading. Later in the book, you will find that there is great opportunity for you in the market place. There's no reason for you to continue struggling. When I speak of hand to mouth, I'm talking about the person with little to no income or investments to speak of. I have turned many would-be investors away who were attempting to invest their grocery money. If you fit that description, I have one piece of advice for you. You have to commit to creating a better life for yourself. Once you do that you need to understand that your commitment needs to be validated by decisive, intentional actions. But before you can take action you need a plan. A written plan, which means you have to be willing to write...or speak into a microphone using a recorder and perhaps dictation software or the recorder on your cel phone. Either way you need to record your goals. You need to be clear about your intentions. The spirit and energy behind this action should resemble the energy displayed in an all-out battle. Think fourth quarter, superbowl, the score's tied and the ball is in your hands. Are you gonna casually approach your opponent...or do you think a bit of aggression would suit the occasion? Visualize, and write out your goals. This is important.

This is your overarching plan for conquest. You can come back later at another time and casually refine your plan as you fill in the details. Right now, you need a major shift. The easiest way to facilitate that shift is through a major shift in your energy coupled with a clear vision energizing your intention. If you can manage to isolate yourself this will be even more powerful! First clearly define your goals. Next see yourself living inside of that vision. If you're home alone or driving down the highway with the windows closed this is the perfect time to speak your new life into existence. "I AM THE BEST DATA MINER TO EVER MINE DATA!!!!!" (or whatever your vocation is) Repeat this mantra over and over and build onto it as you go: "I HAVE SMASHED ALL THE DATA MINING RECORDS TO DATE!!!!!"

If your goal is to be the best, the most legendary human being to ever do whatever it is that you do then scream that to the top of your lungs. You have to understand that you are whatever you say you are and screaming it locks it into the subconscious mind. The legendary producer Mike Todd once said, "Being broke is a temporary situation. Being poor is a state of mind". I would follow that up with this: I have met many struggling people in my life. However, I can count on one hand the number of those people who I would consider actually broken. Think about what it means for something or someone to be broke. Broke means it's done, useless, obsolete, destroyed. A lack of cash or cashflow doesn't make a person obsolete. Understanding that we are who we say we are, it's important to realize that you have to stop referring to yourself as broke. It's ok to say that your funds are low or you have cashflow challenges but broke? Nah... Retire that word from your vocabulary when it comes to how you describe yourself. Companies have cashflow problems all the time. The board members don't sit at the table and say, "we're broke". No, they recognize the problem for what it is and get right down to the business of solving the problem. You must learn to do the same. Identify the problem. Next, focus on the solution, not the problem… The nuggets I've just given you can change the direction of your life, so don't sleep on them... One other important thing to understand is that your lack of money is not your problem. Your lack of a plan is the problem. I'm not talking about an idea. Ideas are good and they generally precede the plan, but a plan is something altogether different. I could write an entire book on this subject alone. But for the sake of brevity, I'll leave you with some recommended readings to help you get unstuck. I encourage you to read "Secrets of the Millionaire Mind" by T. Harv Eker. One of the issues that Eker identifies as a barrier to success for many people is unconsciously, taking on the financial habits of our parents. This is one of the reasons poor people often raise children who become poor adults. Even people who are raised by financially responsible, conservative parents suffer this same fate. I usually laugh when someone tells me that the reason they don't invest money is because they don't believe in taking risks. These same people get in the car and drive 50mph three feet away from other cars moving in the opposite direction at an equivalent rate of speed. If that ain't risky you tell me what is? This proves that everyone has some level of risk tolerance. When it comes to money, risk tolerance is usually dictated by fear more-so than financial wherewithal. The fear is a result of what we were taught to believe about ourselves, our abilities and money. You will risk your life everyday driving to work to earn a pay-check but you won't risk anything at all to become financially independent so that you never have to drive to work again. That's a result of programming... Another great book is Brian Tracy's "Million Dollar Habits". If trauma, abuse or deep-rooted negative programming is at the core of your negative relationship with money, you might consider spending some time focusing on healing. Dr. Joe Dispenza's work, "Tuning in to new potentials" & "Reconditioning the body to a new mind" are both excellent for dealing with this sort of thing. Another great master along the lines of healing and doing away with limiting beliefs and thought patterns is Stanisav Grof. His book, "Healing Our Deepest Wounds: The Holotropic Paradigm Shift" contains techniques that are considered to be miraculously effective by many, including Václav Havel, former president of Czech Republic. Depending on the severity of your condition, you may feel that it's appropriate for you to focus solely on exploring the healing before attempting to address your finances. That's an internal decision that only you are qualified to make. Both Dr. Dispenza and Grof's offerings have the ability to facilitate healing for your purse and every other area of your life. These types of books can serve as medicine for the sickness caused by poverty programming. You've gotta change your thinking and your habits in order generate better cash flow. Once you've managed to create enough cash flow to cover your basic necessities it's time to start planning how to get out front. Now you you're ready to begin putting away money for your future investments.

For someone who's managed to save a small or large amount of money and they wish to deploy that capital into a safely structured, high- yielding asset, I highly encourage them to consider purchasing partials. In a typical partial purchase transaction, the note buyer would identify the number of payments to be purchased at a discount. The note buyer would then become the holder of the entire note until he/she has received all of the projected payments under the terms of the partial purchase agreement. Once the note buyer has received the final payment of the scheduled partial purchase, the note is returned to the original lender and the remaining payments revert back to the original lender. The case study below illustrates precisely what I'm talking about:

Sharon has a $320,000 note and trust deed secured by an office condo in Bellaire, Texas. She's owned the property free and clear since she and her dad constructed it 7 years prior. She sold the property via seller-finance to her insurance agent 4 years ago when he was trying to get his brokerage off the ground. Bryant, the debtor is the owner of a successful insurance franchise. He operates the franchise out of one side of the building and leases the other side to a dentist. The note and trust deed are written in the name of Bryant's LLC without a personal guarantee so there is no way to go after Bryant to collect if for some reason the loan goes into default at some point in the future. We also can't pull credit because the debtor is an LLC with no personal guarantee, which means we have no way of determining Bryant's creditworthiness or ability to repay. On top of that Sharon has not done a good job keeping records of the mortgage payments as she is currently missing proof of payment for two of the past 12 months. So, as far as I'm concerned, Bryant has missed two payments. Bryant may have paid perfectly but we have no way of knowing whether he did or didn't. The property is valued at $400,000 so the equity spread is approximately $80,000 ($400,000 - $320,000 loan balance = $80,000). Sharon is looking to sell the entire note so that she can use the capital to develop another property just south of Houston. The terms of the note are as follows: $320,000 loan, 5% interest per annum payable in monthly installments of $1,717.83 amortized over 30 years.

Sharon Sells to Bryant

Sales price	$360,000
Bryant's down payment	$40,000
Bryant's loan amount	$320,000
Bryant's monthly payment	$1,717.83

Loan terms: $320,000 loan, 5% interest per annum payable in monthly installments of $1,717.83 amortized over 30 years

Sharon has collected $82,455.84 in monthly payments from Bryant over the last 4 years

Sharon found Axiom Note Trade online and filled out the

"request for quote" form via our website. I followed up with a phone call to her to confirm some of the details of the loan. Since I wasn't happy with the way the note was structured, I decided to only offer a partial purchase. Meaning, instead of us purchasing the entire note we would only purchase a set number of payments. In this case we decided to purchase only 60 months worth of payments. Our offer was $45,000 for 60 months of the unpaid balance. The value of those 60 payments was $103,069.80. Sharon was a little disappointed about the pricing until I took the time to educate her on the reasons why my offer was not a full purchase offer. I had to make sure she understood that the relatively low interest rate, coupled with the long amortization (30 years) meant that it would take a longer period of time to get a return on our investment. I explained that the lack of complete pay history and the absence of a personal guarantee really hurt the file. I've found over the years that it really helps to take the time to educate note sellers as opposed to just throwing numbers at them. Once they understand that they're dealing with a professional and not some shady character trying to hustle them out of their investment it's easier to build rapport. I've trained my team to operate this way with each and every phone call.

Sharon agreed to give my offer careful consideration and call back if it seemed like a good fit for her. She called back a few days later and gave me a breakdown of the entire situation. What it came down to for her was something known as the "time value of money". This is a well-known concept in the world of investing. The time value of money (TVM) is the concept that money available at the present time is worth more than the identical sum in the future due to its potential earning capacity.

Sharon's Sells a Partial to Axiom	
Initial property sale	
Property sales price	$360,000.00
Down payment from Bryant	$40,000.00
Loan amount	$320,000.00
Monthly payments	$1,717.83
Sharon Sells partial to Axiom	
Loan balance at time of partial sale	$299,616.00
Partial purch price	$45,000.00 (60 payments worth $103,069.80)

Sharon gets $40,000 at closing and will be entitled to receive 252 payments of $1,717.83 beginning at month 109 after the payments revert back to her. That's a total projected revenue of $555,349 over the life of the loan. If Bryant sells and pays her off early her rate of return goes up. Otherwise, she's got a good steady stream of cash flow to look forward to over the long term

This core principle of money holds that provided money can earn interest, any amount of money is worth more the sooner it is received. In other words, Sharon needed cash right now so that she could move forward on a very lucrative multimillion-dollar deal in another part of town and she was willing to sell at a steep discount because she didn't have any other options for accessing capital without incurring further debt. Sharon had already taken out a home equity loan and borrowed from her retirement savings. She had also taken out a $70,000 loan from her aunt and uncle to raise the capital she needed. So she didn't want to take on any more debt. She and her estate planning attorney had run the numbers and concluded that the projected profit on the new deal was large enough for her to justify all of the steps she'd taken up to this point. But she's exhausted all of her options and was still lacking about $20,000. Sharon was 7 years away from retirement and extremely determined to reach her critical capital goal. Sharon exemplified exactly what I mean when I say," invest with fidelity. She showed a dedication (fidelity) to her investment objective and was willing to stretch a little bit to bring it into fruition. Most people don't have this level of commitment to success.

They will go broke buying luxury cars and high-end clothes so they can look like they are wealthy. But when it comes to actually sitting down, identifying their critical capital needs and plotting a course for success and sticking to the plan no matter what, most people just do not have what it takes. Sharon, on the other hand is not like most people. She knows what she wants and more importantly, how to get it and at this point in life, nothing can stop her. I like Sharon. I think she's an amazing woman in so many ways. Do I think she could've cut herself a better deal with Bryant when she sold him the building? Of course I do! If she had consulted with me going into the deal, I would've encouraged her to double the interest rate. This would have doubled her rate of return and compelled Bryant to either come up with the cash to pay her off sooner or refinance to get a better rate which from Sharon's perspective would have given her the same net result. Since Sharon wrote a loan with a low interest rate and no personal guarantee and the down payment was somewhat small relative to the loan amount, we opted to purchase the note at a low "investment to value ratio" (ITV). Investment to Value refers to the amount of capital invested as a percentage of the property value.

Property Value ÷ Capital invested = Investment to Value (ITV)
\$400,000.00 ÷ \$45,000.00 = 11.25%

The higher the risk a particular note represents the lower your ITV should be. Put another way, the lower the quality of loan the lower your investment in the note should be. Buying partials is one way to lower your ITV and still provide the note seller with the capital they need. Sometimes there are other factors involved that would warrant a reduction in the ITV. Most real estate investors aren't aware of these factors partly because they don't have a background in mortgage finance and have not taken the time to educate themselves on this aspect of the business. I have seen time and time again where this has proven to be a costly mistake. Sharon's situation is a perfect example of what I'm talking about. Her lack of knowledge cost her more than $500,000 over the life of the loan. Had she known; she could have made a change to the note upfront that would've taken her less than 2 seconds to pencil in. Can you imagine how she felt after I pointed this out to her? But this was her first note deal and I doubt it will be her last...

Now let's take a look at Axiom's side of the transaction and see how we did.

Axiom's Partial Purchase

Sharon seller-financed to Bryant – loan amount	$320,000 (360k – 40k = 320k)
Axiom buys a partial – purchase price	$45,000.00
Axiom's investment to value ratio (ITV)	11.25%
Axiom's Yield	33%

Loan Terms: $320,000 at 5% interest per annum payable in monthly installments of $1717.83 amortized over 360 months.

Axiom purchased this note at an 11.25% investment to value (ITV). This is an example of how you as an investor can come in after a loan has already been created and utilize the power of leverage to protect your capital against a possible default in the future.

Axiom's yield (return on investment) in this deal is 33%. That's because we invested substantially less capital into this deal and yet we're receiving the same $1,717.83 monthly payment as Sharon was for her $320,000.00 loan. The original note rate is 5% but we increased our yield over the next 60 months by investing substantially less than the face value of those 60 payments

Axiom invested $45,000 to purchase a stream of payments worth $103,069.80. That's a profit of $58,069.80 created with the stroke of a pen

We invested a small amount of capital and created a profit of over 58k. In this case we chose to go with a partial purchase to mitigate risk. However, partials can be used in cases where you're just starting out investing and your capital is limited. If you only had $45k to invest it wouldn't be hard to find a note holder whose willing to give up a portion of their future payments for a lump sum today.

Now that you understand the power of leverage using partials to minimize risk let's take a look at another scenario where a partial purchase was used to create leverage and help out an investor in need. This one has a few more moving parts.

Sarah had owned this vacant lot looking out over Pacific Beach in Sandiego for nearly 30 years. She had planned to build a beach house on the lot before a car accident left her paralyzed from the waist down some 5 years after she purchased the lot. Sarah still owed approximately $25,282 to her local credit union for the $130,000 loan that she'd taken out 13 years ago using the land as collateral to help with medical expenses. About 8 months ago, John, a builder approached her about buying the lot. John was self-employed and had excellent credit but couldn't get a bank loan because he didn't claim much income when he filed taxes. This is a common problem for entrepreneurs. Sarah and John worked out a deal. John would purchase the lot for $325,000 with $100,000 down payment. The loan would be for $225,000 at 5.5% interest per annum payable in monthly installments of $1,838.44 amortized over 15 years with the final balloon payment of $169,000 due in 5 years. Since Sarah still has $25,000 of an underlying lien on the property and needed all of the $100,000 down payment to pay medical expenses, she would need to do a wraparound mortgage in order to make the transaction work.

Sarah used a "wrap-around mortgage" aka a "wrap". This is a mortgage, trust deed, or land contract that includes a prior loan, called the underlying loan. Here's how it works: A debtor owns or buys a property with a first mortgage on it. Without paying off the first mortgage, the debtor sells the property, creating a mortgage for an amount that includes the amount due on the first mortgage. The new owner makes one monthly payment to the original debtor, out of which the original debtor makes the payment on the first mortgage, keeping the difference for herself.

For example, in this case, Sarah owns the property with a $130,000 first mortgage. She sells the property to John for $325,000 without paying off the first mortgage (after his $100,000 down payment he owes Sarah $225,000). John makes payments to Sarah on the $225,000, out of which Sarah then makes payments on the original $130,000 mortgage. Keep in mind that approximately 13 years have passed since Sarah originally borrowed the $130,000 so it's now paid down to $25,000. The difference between the $25,000 and the $225,000 is called "the equity in the wrap".

Sarah sells property to John

Sarah's balance on underlying lien: $25,000 (original loan $130k paid down to $25k)

Sarah sells to John:	$325,000 (appraised value = Fair Market Value)
John's down payment:	$100,000
Sarah seller-financed to John:	$225,000

Terms of loan: $225,000 at 5.5% interest per annum payable in monthly installments of $1,838.44 amortized over 15 years with the final balloon payment of $169,000 due in 5 years. Even though the loan to John only has a 5.5% face rate Sarah still earned a **ROI of 62.98%** through the first 9 months of the note.

John's payment to Sarah on new loan:	$1,838.44
Sarah's payment to bank on original loan:	$1,028.03 (original loan aka underlying lien)
Sarah's positive cashflow after monthly pymts to cred union:	$810.41

Sarah received $100,000 down payment in addition to the positive cash flow of $810.41 from John with the seller-financed loan using a wrap. For most people $810.41 a month created out of thin air is nothing to snub your nose at…even in California. However, it wasn't quite enough to cover all of her accumulated debt which included some pretty hefty medical bills. She had managed to retire most ofthe debt using the down payment from John, but she needed several more thousand dollars before she could really restore balance to her finances.

In addition to being burdened with the medical bills she desperately needed to figure out a way to pay for repairs and modifications to her home. The ramp leading up to her front door was badly weathered and there were signs that the shower pan in her master bathroom was leaking badly. She wasn't sure if she had a mold problem but there was a constant odor of moisture and mildew coming from the bathroom. Every time Sarah brought up the topic of her deteriorating home her sister and brother-in-law would try to convince her to move into an assisted living facility. Sarah resented the fact that they would even consider asking her to do such a thing. "Those places are for decrepit people who can't do anything for themselves. I'm not old, I just have a disability and I'm not broken…my house is. I'd rather die than give up my house and move into one of those places", she muttered to herself. This had gone on for years and it had just gotten to where she didn't even want to mention the house to her sister. One day while cleaning up her living room she found a letter that she'd received from Axiom offering to buy the note secured by the ocean- front property in San Diego. She really didn't want to give up the steady stream of income that she had become so accustomed to. But she knew she had to do something to come up with the money to make the repairs on her home. Plus she was constantly stressing over the medical bills which had gotten so far out of control that she knew she had to do something…and fast. When Sarah called the office she was very assertive, "hello, this is Sarah Liepold, I received your letter about my note but I only need $60,000. I'm not gonna sell the entire thing. I need you to work with me because I'm in a bind and I have nowhere else to get the money I need to repair my house". We crunched the numbers and here's what we came up with:

After carefully evaluating her note I determined that there were a couple of things about the note that I considered to be unattractive: The thing that stood out like a sore thumb was the fact that the loan was written up at the relatively low interest rate of 5.5%. In addition to that, the loan was secured by vacant land. Apparently, the debtor hadn't quite gotten around to building a house on it yet. Vacant land represents a higher risk in the world of mortgage finance. Also, the loan only had about 8 months of seasoning. Seasoning refers to the number of months that a loan has been in place. In this case the debtor had only been making payments for 8 months. That's well short of what's considered optimal seasoning in the world of seller-financed notes. On the other hand, there were a few redeeming factors to consider about this deal: The debtor had an extremely high credit score; the property was valued at 1.1million dollars which left us with an equity spread of $875,000. Also, with a $100,000 down payment, the debtor did have considerable skin in the game. Those two factors alone made the deal attractive enough for me to stroke the check for the deal, especially considering Sarah only needed $60,000 cash ($25,000 to pay off her underlying loan and about $35,000 for home improvements and medical bills). Sarah accepted our offer to purchase 59 months' worth of payments for $60,483.01 with Axiom paying all closing costs. After we have collected the 59th payment all subsequent payments revert back to Sarah. Those 59 payments are worth $108,467.96 and Axiom purchased them for $60,483.01. Let that sink in for a minute… Here's what that looks like for Sarah:

Sarah's Beach-front Property

Original property purchase: $130,000 (borrowed 130k from credit union)
Sarah's monthly pmt to credit union: $1028.03.55 (130k @ 5% per anum 15 yr loan)
Unpaid loan balance after 13 years; $25,000

Sarah sells her lot to John the builder:$325,000 (sold at fair market value)
Down payment from John: $100,000
Sarah seller-fin to John: $225,000 (5.5% per anum 15 yr loan w/5yr balloon)
9 Monthly payments recvd from John so far:$16,545.96 (Sarah received payments for 9 mos)
Balloon payment due Sarah in 5yrs: $169,400

Sarah sells partial note to Axiom: $60,483.01 (59 payments worth $108,467.96)
Sarah's remaining cash after paying off $25,000 underlying loan:**$35,483.01**

Sarah was able to eliminate the $25,000 unpaid balance on the underlying loan, complete the repairs on her home and had enough cash left over to cover her outstanding medical bills. She'll also receive one more monthly payment of $1,838.44 before collecting the $169,400 balloon payment due in month 60 of the loan.

Obviously, this was a great deal for Sarah. I was happy to be able to assist in her time of need. This is a common theme in our business. It seems most note sellers are either looking for a way to ease their head out of the lion's mouth or they are seeking to free up more capital to take advantage of other business opportunities. Either way, it's always a pleasure to help someone improve their situation.

Making a handsome profit for helping others gives me the feeling of being the engineer of a double blessing. Because we are dealing with amortizing notes that improves all parties position as each month goes by it's kinda like the gift that keeps on giving. I don't know of any other legitimate business in the world that operates this way. Usually, in business there is a consumer/buyer and a producer/ seller of goods or services. The consumer usually purchases something that rapidly decreases in value and the seller walks away with the consumer's hard-earned cash. End of story. Not so in the note business. We are really dealing business to business and executing a transaction that involves an asset that increases in value over time or improves all party's net worth. Everybody wins… Speaking of that, let's see how Axiom made out in this transaction:

Axiom Buys a partial from Sarah	
Partial note purchase	$60,483.01 (59 payments worth $108,467.96)
Property equity position	$875,000 (appraised value minus $225k note)
Axiom's Yield	**26.75%**
Axiom's ROI	**179%**

Even though the loan was only written with an interest rate of 5.5% we were able to realize a yield of **26.75%** because we purchased the note for only $60,483.01 yet we are receiving the same monthly payment of $1,838.44

As you can see, partials are a great way to build wealth investing in notes. Many of our most profitable deals are partial purchase transactions. It's actually my favorite way to purchase notes. One reason is sometimes I don't like the way a particular note is structured or perhaps there's not a sufficient pay history to really gauge the debtor's ability to pay. This is especially true when there's an LLC listed as the debtor with no personal guarantee on the note. Another situation that might warrant me deciding to only purchase a set number of payments would be a loan with an extremely high balance on a single- family residential home. Most note buyers don't like buying large balance loans on single-family homes. I'm speaking of loans at or around the 1 million dollar range and above. This is because you're risking a lot of capital on one note. It's much more prudent to have capital deployed over several smaller loans as opposed to one large loan. If you had a million dollars it would be much safer to have that capital spread out over 10 properties each with a $100,000 loan on each as opposed to one loan of a million dollars. There are a host of other reasons I would opt to purchase a partial over purchasing the entire note. If you are working with limited capital you can use partials to build a very lucrative portfolio of real estate notes.

Now that you understand the power of this strategy it should be easy to see how you can start from wherever you are and begin to create a portfolio of passive income using real estate notes. One ofthe keys to success in building wealth with real estate notes is to do just what Sharon did, "invest with fidelity". That means stay true to your mission even when things get a little challenging. Be creative if you must. Sacrifice where necessary but don't you give up!

In the next chapter I'll show you how to get an excellent rate of return from short term note investments of 3 to 18 months without quitting your dayjob.

CHAPTER 6

QUICK PROFITS WITH PRIVATE MONEY

How to earn big-time returns on short term loans

"My parents always taught me that my day job would never make me rich; it'd be my homework." ~Daymond John

Throughout most of this book, we've looked at real estate note investments that are amortized over longer periods of time; 15, 20 & 30 years. Many of these amortizing loans had balloon features included to shorten the time to maturity and increase the rate of return. The balloon feature is one of the most important aspects of the loan as it ensures that the loan is paid off over a shorter period of time, thus freeing up capital and allowing the investor to redeploy the capital into other investments. Whenever I write a balloon into a loan it's usually a 3, 5 or 7-year balloon. In addition to increasing my rate of return, this allows me to determine how long my money's out there working before I pull it back in and capture my profits.

For some investors, time is more of a factor and they just can't afford to wait 3 to 7 years or more to realize their profits on a deal. These individuals can be a real estate investor's best friend. I say this because real estate investors are often in situations where they have investment properties with excellent profit potential. Many times the real estate investor may have purchase money but they may be lacking money for repairs. In other cases, the investor is seeking purchase money but can cover the repair costs on their own. However, in most cases the investor is looking for purchase and renovation money. In the world of real estate investing the term "other peoples money" or OPM is a foundational principle that's been at the core of real estate investment strategies for many decades. I know many millionaire developers who rarely use their own capital to buy and or renovate properties. Real estate is largely a game of leverage. You either leverage your time, your money or your expertise. The guy who's devoted his time to learning and mastering real estate investment strategies is likely to leverage his expertise. Whereas, the individual who has capital to deploy but doesn't necessarily have the expertise or the time to deal with managing the whole process will leverage his money. When the two come together you have a powerful combination with very few limits as to what they can accomplish.

In a typical short term note investment scenario the subject property is being purchased far below market value. How far below market value is going to depend on location and market demand. In most markets the average investment property is purchased at or below 65 to 75% of fair market value. However, in some markets where demand is high such as some parts of California, DFW and a few other notoriously hot markets around the country investors commonly pay 80% or more of fair market value for properties they plan to flip other investors, hedge funds or retail buyers. It's important to understand local market trends such as appreciation rates, average number of days on market, unemployment rates, average household income, rental rates etc. Having access to this type of information before putting together a marketing plan for locating real estate deals and exit strategy for disposing of the property can make all the difference in the world as to whether you fall short of your goal or knock the skin of the ball so to speak. I co-founded Axiom Direct Mail & Digital

Marketing 12 years ago so reaching the right audience and accessing the data necessary to make informed decisions regarding investing in any market is a part our daily business process. But most investors don't realize that understanding how to identify and exploit market trends is even more important than picking paint colors and knowing how to identify load- bearing walls.

Most real estate investors look at comps to determine what's a good market to invest in. Comps are helpful to have when doing due diligence on a property but they provide only limited perspective if your goal is to develop a plan for creating consistent, predictable results that can be duplicated by multiple individuals on your team. Comps are the result or after effect of market conditions. You need access to the data that can give you valuable perspective on the cause – the driving forces behind the comps. These other datasets I speak of are driving factors that can't be ignored if your goal is to be efficient, prudent and consistently profitable in real estate investing. For instance, the U.S. population has doubled every 50 for the last 200 years. We are currently at a population total of roughly 300 million people. This means that 30 years from now we will be approximately 400 million people and 600 million 50 years from now. Where will these people live? The number 1 driver of appreciation is demographics. Armed with that bit of information it would be reasonable to focus your attention on desirability, affordability and local economic conditions when it comes to mapping out where you want to begin to establish your real estate empire. Even though I know California is experiencing a real estate goldrush so to speak, I would steer clear of some parts of California unless I'm a flipper. It's not a sustainable economy for long-term hold. This is primarily because of California's long-standing tradition of fiscally irresponsible elected officials. These politicians have done irreversible damage to California's financial system. Let's take a quick look at the state of the Golden State:

- California currently has 4 million pension beneficiaries (this number exceeds the total of 22 states) with unfunded pension debt in excess of 769 billion dollars – Hoover Inst.
- California has the highest income tax rate & 10 highest sales tax rate
- Highest debt-to-income ratio in the country – smartasset.com
- Dead last among U.S. states for quality of life – US News
- According to demographer Joel Kotkin "the state is run for the very rich, the very poor and public employees"
- According to a 2017 Harvard Univ report 1/3 renters in LA are severely rent burdened, "meaning they spend at least half their income on housing"
- According to a 2015 report by Standard & Poors, a shift in the stock market from gains to losses could obliterate California's budget because over half the states revenue comes from the wealthiest 1%
- According to a 2018 report by CNBC California is losing more and more resident's each year due to domestic migration as a result of the constant increase in the cost of living
- California counties levy an asset tax on businesses. This is unattractive for economic development

I could go on and on. I know the weather's beautiful and there are many attractions that will make California a popular destination for years to come. But when you consider all of the above along with the almost perpetual wildfires and mudslides it's easy to see why I say California may not be the best market for long-term hold real estate investors unless they're into high-end luxury homes or perhaps low income rentals (the poor have to have a place to live). Then again, low income properties in California can sometimes be priced in the one million dollar range. I don't see the logic in investing one million dollars just to cash flow $3000 per month. You could take that same million and leverage it ten times over in more stable markets, achieve better equity spreads while maintaining a higher level of safety in your portfolio. Besides, much of the appreciation in California has created what we call "soft equity" in the note industry. Soft equity has a tendency to disappear rapidly in a market correction. If you own real estate in California and that real estate is leveraged (meaning you are the debtor on a mortgage) unless you are in a really strong equity position you need to get out now. Otherwise, you will get burned in a market correction. This is just one example of how important it is to have knowledge of local market conditions before deciding on location and investment strategy. Other areas of the country that I would stay away from in terms of long-term hold are primarily in the Northeast, Mid-Atlantic and the Midwestern states. Americans have been fleeing cold, damp and snowy areas for the sunny states for years now. There's no shortage of data available to support that statement.

As far as attractive places to invest going forward, you can't go wrong if you just follow the sun. The data supports a robust population surge in Western states such as Arizona, Nevada as well as the Sunbelt and along the I-85 corridor between Raleigh, NC and Atlanta, Ga. These are just my opinions and are in no way meant to serve as a guide as to where one should invest. I invest in properties and notes nationwide. I own notes in California, but the notes are all short-term maturity notes with substantial hard equity. Hard equity is the amount of the debtor's down payment (aka: skin in the game).

There are 3 main factors that effect housing prices. Below is an outline of those factors and sources for obtaining data related to each:

1. Housing supply
2. Housing demand
3. Housing affordability

Where to FindInfoon Housing Supply

Inventory

- ✓ US Census Bureau
- ✓ National Association of Realtors (NAR)
- ✓ Local Board of Realtors

✓ **New home construction starts**

- ✓ US Census Bureau
- ✓ Local Home Builders Association

Where to find information on Housing Demand

- **Local Employment Situation**
  - http://BLS.gov
  - **Local Investor Activity**
  - **Local Board of Realtors**
- **Consumer Confidence (emotion)**
- **University of Michigan Consumer Confidence Observations**

Where to FindInfoon Housing Affordability

- **Housing Affordability Index**
- **NAR**

✓ **Interest Rate Market & Lending Guidelines**

✓ **Affordability for a Specific Scenario**

✓ **Rent vs. Buy Calculator**

I won't go into a long dissertation about how all these factors come into play with regards to home pricing…that would be the topic of a whole different book. Obviously, it would benefit anyone to learn all they can about the various factors that support and exert pressures on the market that she's investing in. However, you don't need to be an economist or real estate expert to win big investing in real estate notes. I suggest that you learn all you can and put together a team of reliable experts to help cover your blind spots. If you have investment capital to deploy passively and can team up with a reliable real estate note investor with the knowledge and experience of how to successfully acquire and exit a real estate deal you may just find that you're in a position to churn quick profits over and over multiple times each year.

At Axiom we work with regular people who want to deploy capital on a short term basis and help them to generate double-digit returns.

Below is a sample deal to illustrate how this private lender strategy might work.

Axiom identified an investment property in the city of Stonecrest, a suburb of Atlanta, Ga. Jasmine, the seller is motivated, meaning she wants to sell and doesn't care about making a profit. She just wants to rid herself of the headache of owning the house. You see, the house has a roof leak which is really just a leak around the seal or boot at the base of the hot flue stack. This is basically a vent pipe extending up through the roof from the hot water tank. Jasmine has paid several shade tree handyman types and jack-leg plumbers to climb up on the roof to repair the leak over the years. A couple of them managed to provide temporary relief using improper material and substandard techniques but somehow the water eventually always seems to find its way back into her living room. There's also a persistent leak underneath the kitchen sink that her boyfriend can't seem to fix. They've just resigned to the notion that the sink is unfixable and the only remedy is to keep a bucket underneath the sink to catch the water so that the defective sink doesn't cause further damage in the basement. The basement smells of must and mildew. Jasmine is certain that the moisture odor is coming from the leaky kitchen sink. What she doesn't know is that she actually has a foundation leak. Because the grade of the lot that her house sits on slopes away from the foundation the damage from the foundation leak is minimal and the basement only takes on a small amount of water during really heavy rains. Why does any of this matter to us? Well, Jasmine owns the house free and clear and the homes in her neighborhood sell for 300-400k. Jasmine is looking for a new beginning somewhere… anywhere other than where she currently lives. When I went to inspect the home, Jasmine was quick to inform me that she didn't have time for games. "I know it's a dump. I need $70,000 dollars to buy a condo in the city. If you can make that happen we can talk. If not, let the doorknob hitcha where the good lord splitcha!

I stopped in my tracks and looked at her. I was shocked! Jasmine was loud and assertive. I wondered if she was joking because she wore a half-smirk on her face. But she wasn't, she was serious. I smiled back. "I think we might be able to make that work. But I'll need to have a look around. Is that ok with you?" I asked. She nodded in approval. It took me a bit longer to inspect this house because I didn't want to have to schedule a second inspection. Jasmine works two jobs and only gets one day off per week on one of her jobs. It had taken us almost 3 weeks to align our schedules so that she could meet us to open the house for inspection today. Below is what my inspection revealed.

Jasmine's House Rehab Cost	
Repair seals around boots	$275
Gut and install new kitchen cabinets, flooring, sink and appliances	$10,000
Renovate 3 ½ bathrooms	$7,000
Refinish hardwood floors through main level, new carpet in basement	$4,500
Repair foundation wall	$5,000
Pain interior	$3,000
Install new water tank	$900
Pressure wash exterior brick	$350
Install new plants - landscaping	$700
Total rehab cost	**$31,725**

The roof on Jasmine's house had 30-year architectural shingles. It had at least a good 15 years of life remaining. Apparently, whoever installed the shingles did a good job. The vent extending up from the water tank had been damaged and had come unseated by the jack legged plumber in his attempt to repair the water tank. In the process, he damaged the seal and that's what caused the leak. This leak was the crux of her desire to abandon the house… Had it not been for that jack legged plumber Jasmine might have never considered selling Axiom the house. I owe that guy a debt of gratitude.

I sat down in the living room, right next to the bucket beneath the leaky roof and wrote out a simple, one- page purchase agreement. Jasmine was eager to sign.

After checking comparable sales within a 1mile radius and driving to look at the comps I determined that a conservative value for this property after all repairs and improvements have been completed would be $350,000. At that price point the average number of days on the market is 65 days. That means that a properly renovated property in this neighborhood listed for $350k should take no longer than 65 to 70 days to sell. With our in-house marketing platform we typically retail houses in about half the time it takes to sell a house on the MLS. Here are the numbers for the note deal we offered to our private lender.

Short term note deal Jasmine's house

Property purchase price	$70,000
Renovation cost	$31,725
Closing costs	$5,000
Total loan amount	**$106,725** (12 mos. @ 10% Interest only)
After Repaired Value (ARV)	**$350,000**
Lender ITV	**30%**

Loan Terms: $106,725.00 @ 10% interest only. Interest accrued monthly with payment of accrued interest and principle due and payable upon maturity in 12 months. That's a profit of $10,672.50 for our short term note investor in under 12 months.

The short term note investor gets a note and security deed the same as the note investors from the examples earlier in the book or any bank would get for a mortgage loan. It provides a full and direct legal title transfer from the borrower to the lender, leaving the equitable title with the borrower. The lender then provides the loan.This provides safety and security for the note investor's capital for the duration of the loan.

MJ, our private note investor was happy to jump on this one. We waited 3 weeks to close in order to give Jasmine time to find a temporary place to live until she could find her condo in the city. MJ's profit was $10,672.50 in interest plus a $10,000 exit fee when we closed on the sale of the renovated house. That's a 19% ROI. I offered the additional exit fee to sweeten the pot since I knew that we stood to gain a considerable profit on this deal in a short period of time. Axiom netted $222,602.50. The renovation took about 6 weeks and we immediately began marketing the property for sale as soon as it was presentable. It took us 45 days from the day we started marketing the property to find a buyer and we closed 30 days later. Our short-term loan program allows for similar and sometimes better returns on smaller investments.

There are a number of ways that I go about making sure that my private lender/partners receive above average ROI. The "Exit Fee" in the example above is just one of them. There are many ways to structure a deal. I typically choose the structure based on the specifics of the investment and the preference of the lender/partner involved in the deal. In this type of transaction, the most important thing, next to ROI is making sure that all the documents clearly spell out that my investor/partner gets paid first in any and all scenarios. Afterall, she/he is putting up all the capital so it's only right that they receive nothing less than the highest level of protection.

In the next chapter, I will provide several examples of how you can obtain the funds to start building a portfolio of passive income using real estate notes if you don't have enough in your bank account to get started today.

CHAPTER 7

WHERE TO FIND INVESTMENT CAPITAL

"Start by doing what's necessary; then do what's possible; and suddenly you are doing the impossible". -Francis of Assisi

In this chapter, I'm going to show you where you can get the money to invest in real estate notes. No matter who you are, you can start investing in notes right away, even if you don't have enough in your bank account to get started today.

Earlier in the book, I talked about moving or rolling capital from your 401k or traditional IRA's into a self- directed IRA as a way of accessing investment capital. For most Americans, who don't have liquid cash in the bank or under the mattress this is the most viable option for quickly accessing investment capital. But what if you don't have a retirement savings account? What if you don't have much cash under your mattress or sitting in your regular savings account? These are common questions I hear whenever I'm speaking to people at REIA and meetup groups. My answer to these questions is always, "How far are you willing to go looking for the money?" You see, most people subscribe to the scarcity model, which is the complete opposite of the reality that I live in. I subscribe to the abundance model. In a nutshell, the abundance model is based on the premise that there is an abundance of everything we need all around us...including money. And our access to it is limited only by our thinking. For instance, most people only expect to earn money by punching a clock. Or going into the office and performing based on a job description that someone else has laid out for them. I call that trading time for dollars. If you buy into the abundance model you get to create your own job description. And…you can have multiple job descriptions. Your ability to grasp the concept I'm laying out for you right now is really the biggest determining factor of whether or not you're able to live life on your terms as an investor. It's your belief in ability to meet your goal of reaching your critical capital needs and creating wealth for yourself regardless of the obstacles that may stand before you. Remember Jasmine? All she wanted was peace of mind. To her, peace of mind could only be found within the confines of a condo in the city. I would argue that she could've found peace of mind inside the four walls of the place she had called home for so many years. But she couldn't see past the stains from the drip of the leaks underneath the sink and the roof. But you and I know that those things are minor inconveniences that can easily be solved with the stroke of a pen. Jasmine didn't realize this because she was relying on bad information from substandard tradesmen. She thought she was saving money by hiring cheap labor to repair her home. In reality, those guys cost her almost $300,000. So, she saved a few hundred dollars on the repair cost only to give away 1000 times that on the sale of the property. It's all a matter of perspective. She didn't think that she could come up with the money to repair the roof and the sink and all the other things that were wrong with the house. Jasmine had a TV hanging on her living room wall that's worth more than all the electronic devices in most peoples' houses. She drove an expensive luxury car. She had so many new name brand clothes with the tags still on them that her closets were overflowing. I'm not judging Jasmine for liking nice things. My goal is to point out that she could've made a few sacrifices and curbed her appetite for expensive things and walked away from that house $300,000 richer. I don't think there's anything wrong with a person working for what they want and going out there and getting it. But for me it's a question of what are you sacrificing to own expensive clothes and drive that flashy car? This is what held Jasmine back and diminished her wealth significantly. She had developed a lifestyle of form over function. There's a cultural phenomenon in America of people wearing and driving all of their money. It's self-sabotage.

But this isn't really about Jasmine, It's about you. What's holding you back? Can you pinpoint one area in your life where a subtle tweak…one minor adjustment could open up a world of possibilities that wasn't available to you before? It's all a matter of mindset.

So I ask you, is your mind tuned to the frequency of wealth? Or, is it tuned into the 70" TV hanging on your wall? If you can see yourself executing one of the strategies I've outlined so far in this book then you too are a member of the abundance collective. If not, maybe you should take some time to recalibrate your thinking. It's the only way to move beyond the boundaries of scarcity and break away from limiting beliefs.

Like it stated before, money is all around you. If you have a 401K or traditional IRA, depending on your account balance you may already have all the funds you need to start buying notes. I would strongly suggest that you consider rolling that money into a self-directed account so that you can begin to take control of your own financial future. Don't leave it in the hands of the Wallstreet money masters. They've already gutted many of your pensions, don't allow them to continue to feed on your retirement savings too. There are many companies available to assist you with doing this. It's not difficult at all.

Some of the sources of money that are closest to you in proximity could be members of your own family. We'll explore other options later in this chapter but before we get into any of that I want you to consider the people closest to you. I couldn't think of a better place to start. I was a mortgage banker for many years and I recall vividly seeing family members stroke large checks to help loved ones with down payments to purchase homes. Before you dismiss the idea I want you to think about it for a minute. It's common practice in America for people to reach into their savings and hand over huge chunks of cash to help their kids, grandkids and other relatives acquire a mortgage to purchase a home. I think it's a noble gesture and what not but let's be honest – what they're really doing is contributing to the creation of a massive amount of debt. The type of debt that lasts about as long as herpes. I say this because once most Americans venture into the world of homeownership, they're there to stay. Even if they refinance that loan all they're doing is swapping one debt instrument for another. If they should happen to sell some years later there's almost always another home purchase to follow. You rarely see someone sell there home without ever buying another one. For most people mortgage debt is perpetual. Along with that debt comes a certain degree of risk. They could suddenly become unemployed or suffer a debilitating illness or any number of things could bring misfortune to their doorsteps. Yet people still dig deep and give generously in the name of love to help their loved ones achieve acquisition indebtedness in spite of this risk. And let's face it, a house that's not generating income is a liability. A liability with a huge price tag! It's so ingrained in our culture that it's almost become a tradition. It's so commonplace that we don't even see it for what it is…a liability. Don't get me wrong, I'm a huge proponent of homeownership. The point here is if your loved ones will give you money to assist you in going into debt what's so wrong with seeking their assistance in acquiring an asset? Especially if you plan to use that asset to generate more capital to acquire more assets. I've had this conversation with many of my students over the years and to this day it's a mystery to me where some of the myths about tax liabilities associated with gifting money come from.

For instance, it's a widely held myth that there are huge tax consequences to people who receive gifts from family members. First let me remind you that I'm not a tax professional and I am in no way attempting to give tax advice or any type of advice in this book. I'm simply sharing information that may be helpful to some. But it is my understanding that there is never an instance where the recipient of a gift is subjected to having to pay a gift tax. Regardless of who the giver is or the amount of the gift, there is no such thing in the federal tax code as a gift tax on monetary gifts received from another individual. There are certain scenarios where the person giving monetary gifts are subject to a gift tax. The last time I checked that tax rate was something to the tune of 45% but that only applies to about 1% of the population. Here's why:

Option 1 – The gift that keeps on giving

At the time of the writing of this book there are two circumstances where a gift-giver does not have to pay taxes on the gift:

Annual Gift Tax Exclusion

1. ***When using the annual gift tax exclusion*** - The annual tax exclusion allows for any individual to gift any otherindividual up to 15k per year. There is no requirement for the two individuals to be related by blood or in any other way. (The idea that the two parties have to be immediate family members is one of the most common misconceptions).
2. This 15k annual exclusion is replenishable. Meaning

you could meet a stranger in a back ally once a year and give him 15k each year for the rest of your life and would never have to pay taxes on it (unless of course you lived to be 746 years old…)

3. Married couples each have their own separate annual gift tax exclusion, which means both husband and wife each can give 15k to anyone they choose once a year
4. This means that you and your wife could each receive a 15k gift from your mother and your father on the same day. This would be a total of 60k dollars

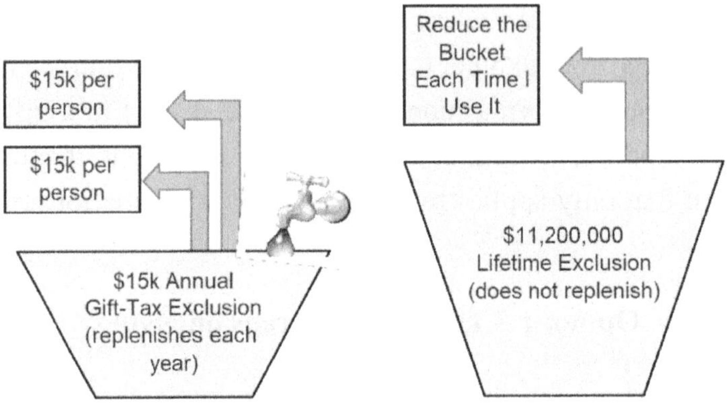

Option 2 The gift that keeps on giving

1. ***When using Lifetime Gift Tax Exclusion*** – The lifetime gift tax exclusion is 11.2 million dollars. That 11.2 million dollars is above & beyond the annual 15k gift tax exclusion. So even though your 15k annual exclusion renews itself each year it still counts against your lifetime gift tax exclusion. What that means is each time you give a gift of 15k that amount is subtracted from your lifetime limit. If you give a gift that exceeds the 11.2-million-dollar amount then you are subject to gift tax. This is why

99% of Americans have no reason to be concerned about the gift tax.

2. There is no limit to the marital exclusion. Meaning if you're worth $100 million when you die and you leave all your assets to your spouse she/he will not have to pay gift tax
3. If you leave the 100 million to someone other than your spouse the federal gift tax exclusion kicks in and your estate would have to pay taxes on the difference between the 11.2 million exclusion threshold and the 100 million that you gifted them
4. Portability – Your allowed to port over the 11.2 million lifetime exclusion to a spouse which means that upon your demise his/her lifetime exclusion bumps up to 22.4 million

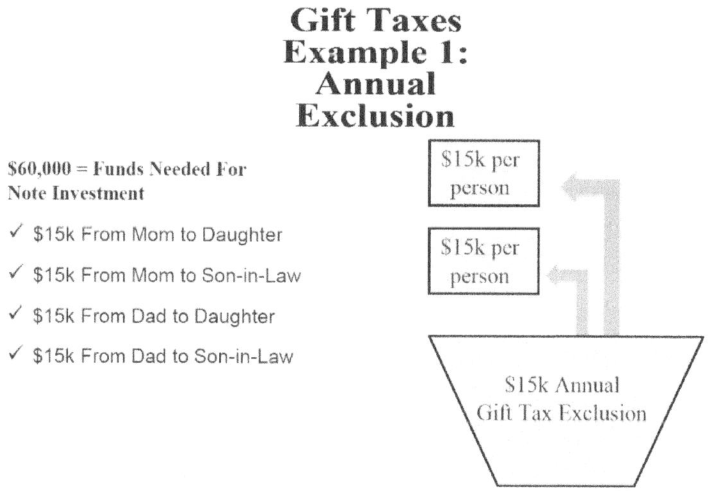

As you can see from the example above, the federal tax code allows us a significant amount of latitude to be creative when it comes to gifting money without triggering a taxable event. Let's look at how we can combine the 15k annual exclusion and the 11.2-million-dollar lifetime exclusion to meet our investment goals where higher levels of liquidity are required:

In the example below Sandy needed $200k to purchase a home with a fair market value FMV of $280k. He and his wife reached out to his parents for help. Sandy's a great guy with a good head on his shoulders, so is his wife so of course, mom and dad said yes.

Gift Taxes Example 2: Lifetime Exclusion

$200,000 = Funds Needed To Purchase Property to resell via Seller-Finance

- ✓ $15k From Mom to Daughter
- ✓ $15k From Mom to Son-in-Law
- ✓ $15k From Dad to Daughter
- ✓ $15k From Dad to Son-in-Law

$200,000

\-

$60,000

=

$140,000

Sandy's parents gifted he and his wife the $200k (60k from the annual exclusion bucket and the other 140k came out of the lifetime exclusion bucket)

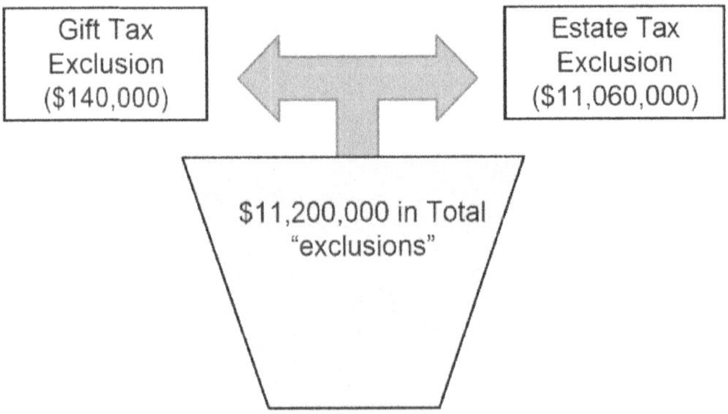

Federal Gift Tax

① Two Buckets of Exclusions

② No Tax to Gift Recipient

③ No Relationship Required

Federal Estate Tax

① Unlimited Marital Exclusion

② $11,200,000 Exclusion (2018)

③ Many States Have Lower Limits

④ Portability

Portability for Surviving spouse

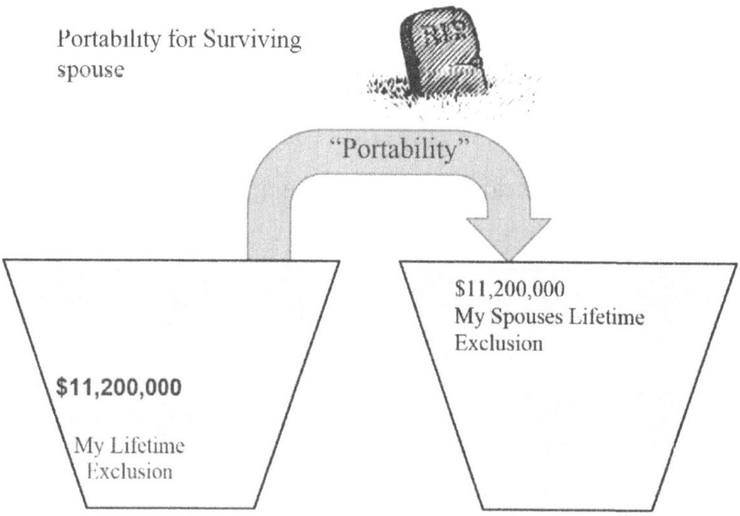

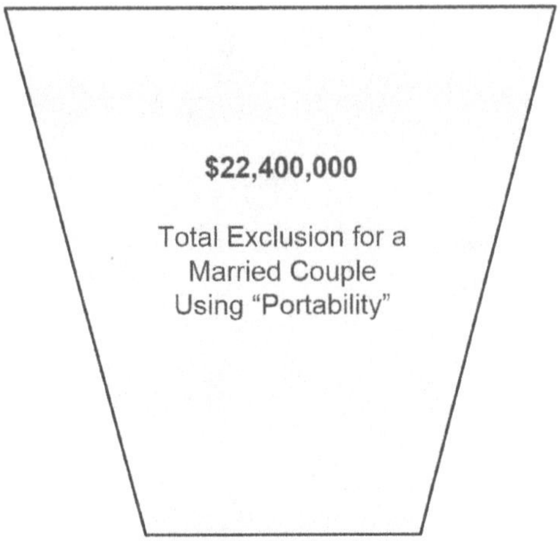

Now that you see how the gift tax exclusions work you can approach mom and dad with confidence to ask for the money you need to build your investment portfolio. The conversation might go something like this, "Mom-Dad, instead of giving me money to acquire debt that I'll owe to the bank for the next 30 years I'd prefer that you gift me the capital to acquire assets so that I can become the bank". The best part about it is you can sleep well at night knowing that you didn't create an additional tax burden for mom and dad.

Option 2 – Personal Loan

If you ask your mom and dad or another relative to gift you the money you need to start investing, they may just whip out the checkbook and start writing before you can get the question out good. On the other hand, they may just tell you to to kick rocks. There are a lot of people out there who don't believe in giving away money under any circumstances…not even to their kids or grandkids. They believe that all money should be earned or borrowed and paid back with interest. I have no judgment when it comes to peoples' personal philosophies about giving money and you shouldn't either. If you have relatives who hold these views perhaps you are in an even better situation than the person who can go to their uncle and get a $200,000 gift. I say this because most people will lend way more money than they would ever consider giving away. The other thing to consider is your relatives will most likely charge a lower interest rate than you can get anywhere else and they won't even care to ask what your credit score is. If you can articulate a plan or present loan terms that are attractive enough for your uncle Russ, you may just find that you have a business partner for life.

I won't go into any long drawn out examples of how to create a profitable loan arbitrage with your family members. I've given you the blueprint in previous chapters of what an attractive loan might look like. All you have to do is figure out what's an acceptable rate of return for him and create a loan with an end buyer that gives you an attractive yield and viola you'll be making big money before you know it!

Option 3 – A Line of Credit

When I say apply for a line of credit you may be thinking that I'm talking about walking into a bank and requesting a credit line. If you qualify and can get approved, by all means, go for it! Bank loans usually require you to jump through a whole lot of hoops to obtain a little bit of money. Usually, the people who are able get large loans from banks are the ones who really don't need the money. The banking system in America is designed to serve the wealthy and feed off everyone else. I noticed years ago that there was a huge void in the marketplace for real estate investors seeking capital to fund deals. I'm not talking about hard money there's plenty of that out there. I'm talking about private money designed to provide small builders and real estate investors the capital they need to take advantage of investment opportunities in the market. That's one of the reasons Axiom offers lines of credit for real estate investors/builders starting at $500k and can be used to purchase multiple properties at once.

This program is very unique to the marketplace. It's all about leverage. There is a minimum credit score of 620 and you must have a minimum 50k liquid cash to qualify. This is an excellent loan program for beginning and seasoned investors alike. Here are the basic guidelines:

- Loans for non-owner occupied residential investment properties
- Drawn balance options available
- Exposure limits up to 10MM for experienced investors
- Loans from $50K to $2MM
- Rates as low as 6.75%
- Financing for Foreign Nationals and Non-Permanent Residents
- Exposure limits and loans up to $500K for beginner investors
- Funding up to: 90% of purchase price 100% of rehab or construction 75% LTV

This is a one of a kind program for the serious investor. But you may find that reaching out to the people in your family and circle of friends gives you access to more capital, better interest rates or maybe even a tax-free gift.

I've given you three great options for obtaining the capital you need to start investing today. There's no room for excuses. Remember, it's all about mindset.

In the next chapter I will reveal the insider secrets of the real estate note business that it took me over 25 years to learn. It's what I call the "best practice note rubric". Follow it and you will be able to structure and analyze note deals like a seasoned professional.

CHAPTER 8

HOW TO STRUCTURE AND ANALYZE REAL ESTATE NOTES LIKE A SEASONED PROFESSIONAL

> *"There's no greater question than "What if", when you're in the moment and non more trivial when the moment has passed"*
> *~ Stan Steele*

In this chapter, I will share with you the in-house rubric that we use in my company to educate team members and investment partners on evaluating real estate notes. This is one of the documents that we use in training to make sure that we maintain a portfolio of high-quality notes. Many note investors purchase solely based on yield with no concern for the quality of the asset. I'm sure that most of those guys consider themselves successful investors. I say happy hunting and continued success to them all. However, I've learned over the years that it's possible and more profitable to build a portfolio of high-quality, high-yielding notes without sacrificing quality. We have a proven system in place for evaluating and originating high-quality notes. We don't have to dedicate resources to chasing down payments and dealing with defaults. It's all about due diligence and attention to detail. There is a certain level of risk associated with any and all forms of investing. However, unlike most other investments, a real estate note is an asset that's backed by another asset...real estate. That's why even if a debtor stops paying and the asset goes dark the brick and mortar that's securing the note does not begin to lose value. This makes note investing a more secure form of investing than anything else in the world. Stocks lose value. I have friends who's stock portfolios have lost so much that they actually had a negative valuation. I've been to some of the worst neighborhoods in the country and even in those neighborhoods I've never seen a piece of real estate that was valued at zero or a negative dollar amount. Gold is a great form of investing and it does hold value over time but gold can be stolen from you. Even if you could pick a house up off its foundation and steal it, you'd have to go down to the courthouse, erase my name from the deed book and back-date it to show yourself as the owner and we all know that's impossible.

It doesn't matter how safe and protected my asset is if it's a worthless, poorly structured instrument. The value is created upfront. My mentor taught me years ago that great notes are usually created not purchased. I couldn't agree more. That's why I'm sharing this document with you. So that you can create your own system for producing high-quality, high-yielding notes over and over again. And should decide to purchase a note from someone else, you'll have guidelines that you can use to make sure that your hard-earned money is protected. There is much more to learn when it comes to creating notes than I could ever squeeze into this one document but it gives you a great foundation to build on. If your desire is to enter the business, you can use this rubric to do it the right way and operate at a high level.

by Stan Steele, CMPS

Chapter 8

How To Evaluate a Note Deal Like a Seasoned Professional

Rubric for Note Structuring & Tips That Yield Bigger Profits

Get the App—Be sure to get a full application. You'll need debtor's SSN for tax reporting and to send out 1098 mortgage interest statements each year so the debtor can use it to get mortgage interest deduction when they file taxes should they decide to itemize. Also, this information is extremely useful if you ever decide to sell thenote. You should check the credit prior to extending a loan to a homeowner. Offering a note for sell without knowing the debtor's credit score is like selling a car without knowing the mileage. By the way, Per the Fair Credit Reporting Act of 1971 any creditor can review a credit report at any time of any of their existing debtors.

When the debtor signed the promissory note, they became the debtor and will remain the debtor until the loan is satisfied.

Per this same Act, the creditor can also grant permission to any investor to review a credit report of the debtor if it is for the purpose of investing in the existing loan between the debtor and creditor.

LTV – LTV, or loan-to-value, refers to how much mortgage you have in relation to how much your property is worth. This is expressed as a percentage. Make sure that the Loan to Value (LTV) is based on TRUE "fair market value" FMV as determined by realistic comparable sales (comps), Broker's Price Opinion (BPO) or appraisal. This is especially important if there is a significant difference between the debtors purchase price and what the person he/she bought the property from paid for it initially in a "quick turn" transaction. A "quick turn" transaction is when a real estate investor buys a house and resells it quickly to an owner occupant or another investor. This is also known as house flipping. A lot of real estate investors sell properties at prices above FMV to unsuspecting buyers. They do this either because they didn't want to pay for the repairs necessary bring the house up to FMV or sometimes they inflate the price out of greed.

DTI – Try to keep the debt to income ratio (DTI) as close to 31/43 as possible. However, if you're purchasing a note that was created by someone else and there was an acceptable down-payment, seasoning and good pay history it could still be a very good note even if the DTI is a little higher due to some of the debtor's income not showing on paper

Credit score - Although we buy notes with scores as low as 500, higher scores usually equals a higher valuation. Keep in mind that if you ever decide to sell your note the credit score makes up about 30 to 35% of the value

Personal Guarantee – If the debtor opts to use a corporate structure such as an LLC or perhaps a Trust to take title to the property be sure to require them to personally guarantee the loan. Without a personal guarantee a potential note buyer cannot pull credit.

When there is no credit or when we can't pull credit we automatically assign a 550 credit score to the debtor. In most cases this cheapens your loan and could be a deal killer depending on the type of property, quality of loan etc. Again, the credit score makes up 30-35% of the value of the note… **Down Payment** – Down payment should be at least 10% of the purchase price. Zero Down and low down payment loans represent a higher risk pro I always require a higher discount when purchasing notes with zero or low down payment.

Payment records - Keep copies of all checks/money orders. If mailed keep copy of envelope it was mailed in. If the debtor pays you in cash don't delay in depositing those funds and be sure to separate that cash from any other cash that you are depositing into your bank account that day. This way a potential note buyer can look at a redacted bank statement and see clear evidence of consistent on time monthly payments.

Late Payments - Be sure to collect late fees as per the terms of the note if they pay late..., If you fail to enforce the terms of your note someone who buys it in the future does not have the right to come in and start charging late fees either and you are likely to have a difficult time selling such a loan.

Hazard Insurance – Require the debtor to maintain a homeowner's insurance policy and make sure that you, the lender are listed as "additional Loss Payee" on the homeowner's insurance policy

Title Insurance Policy – Always get a "Lenders' title policy" at closing, even if you've owned the property for years prior to selling it. This is one of the most important aspects of the note...

Interest Rate – In my opinion Interest rates should be set at a level to provide the desired ROI. Interest rates are generally determined based the desired yield relative to the cost of capital and should also be sufficient enough to offset the level of risk represented by the debtor. I've created a matrix that we utilize on a daily basis to determine the best interest rate to charge on each loan for optimization of safety and ROI. You shouldn't structure a seller- financed note to try and match the prime rate. I've seen many real estate investors make this mistake. In most privately held mortgages the debtor represents a higher risk and the interest rate should be set at a level to offset some of that risk. This helps the debtors by encouraging them to improve their credit rating and refinance as quickly as possible to get a lower rate. In our office we provide every debtor a one on one consultation and documentation to illustrate how a future refinance to a lower interest rate can create an improvement in their cash-flow and accelerate the increase in their equity position. We do this with side by side loan comparisons showing the difference in the amount of their current/proposed monthly payment v/s what their payment could look like if they refinanced to obtain a better rate. We provide the borrower with an in-depth explanation of the amortization table, require homeowners insurance policy and give referrals to reputable credit repair companies. We also place each loan with a servicing company who reports all monthly payments to the three major credit bureaus. This is a tremendous value to the debtor/new homeowner and also helps us by allowing us to create a much safer, more attractive and profitable note should we decide to sell in the future.

Seasoning – Seasoning refers to the length of time the loan has been in place. In other words, if the loan was originated (created) 6 months ago then the loan has 6 months of seasoning. My company purchases notes with as little as 30 days seasoning. Still, the more seasoning a loan has the more valuable it is.

Property Type/Use- The type of property and or the way the property is being utilized by the debtor weighs heavily when pricing the note. For example: If you owned an old, tiny cement block building located on a side street in a very rural, low density population area and decided to seller-finance it to someone who in turn slapped paint on the outside and turned it into a bar, a potential note buyer might look at the structure and have some reservations about their ability to resell that building in the event of a default because of the location, type of property and the way it's being used. The note-buyer might make the assumption that not many people would be willing to pay X amount of dollars to purchase that structure. Therefore, if the note-buyer does make an offer to purchase your note the pricing will likely reflect a deeper discount to offset the risk. Another example of how the property type could negatively affect the value of the note is with regards to mobile homes. Not to be confused with manufactured homes, mobile homes are technically considered automobiles. As such they tend to lose value over time much the same way that a car or truck does. Not do to the mileage but due to depreciation based on salvage value, cost, and estimated useful life of the vehicle.

Therefore, any note transaction involving a mobile home would need to include the land and would be evaluated based on the land value, use and location as opposed to the structure itself. I created a property type/use guide for our staff to use when considering taking a note into our portfolio.

Note Storage—When you finance a property the single most important document you possess is the promissory note. You must maintain possession of the original note throughout the life of the loan. If you lose it you have no means of enforcing the agreement and nothing to sell. You can't sell your note if you don't have a note. In the event of a lost note you can complete and have the debtor sign a notarized "Lost Note Affidavit" You should maintain a copy of the note in a separate location from the original. This copy will be your saving grace should you ever lose the original, decide to sell or have a need to enforce the terms of the note in the future. I suggest using a or a safety deposit box to store the original note.

Servicing

Pay a servicing company to collect payments. There are several really good servicing companies around the country that will service your notes for pennies on the dollar (between $12 to $35/mo). They will not only collect payments for you. They also:

-Send out monthly statements
-send late notices
-send end of year 1098 statements and handle tax reporting
-handle foreclosure proceedings
-monitor taxes and homeowners' insurance and notify you of tax delinquencies or defaults do to missed premiums
-report payment history to the credit reporting agencies, which helps the debtor to build credit

The bottom line is writing quality loans at the point of origination will allow you to command top dollar when it's time to sell. I've covered the most important factors here but there are other considerations. As you can see, there are many things to take into account when creating or evaluating seller-financed loans. It can be a bit of a daunting task if you've never done this type of thing before. Many of my clients that it's a much easier process to just purchase notes from me. They understand that my 25+ years of experience as a real estate investor, mortgage banker and note trader is a great asset to them. They don't have to worry about dotting the "i's" and crossing the "t's". That's my job. Their job is to sit back and collect money.

CHAPTER 9

PREPARING FOR YOUR BEST WORST-CASE SCENARIO

"Every success story begins with people who know what they want to achieve". ~ Napoleon Hill

In this chapter, I'd like to discuss something that most people don't give a whole lot of thought to, Long-term Healthcare (LTHC). This is a topic that no one wants to think about but in my opinion, it's waste of time to discuss wealth building or retirement planning without accounting for the possibility that you or your loved one could someday face health challenges that require you to need long-term healthcare. You may feel that you have superior genes or a lifestyle and dietary habits that have you knocking on the door of immortality. Have you considered however the possibility of a serious accident, medical malpractice or communicable disease? Most people assume that they will live out their lifetime in good health and grow old gracefully. I say this because in all my years of working in the financial services industry I've rarely encountered clients with adequate life insurance and almost never encounter clients with long-term healthcare insurance policy. We all know that life insurance is a must have but most people that I speak with about investments and retirement savings admit that they've never given a single thought to the need for LTHC. I will assume that most of you reading this book fit within this category as well. This is a potential crisis of monumental proportions waiting to happen. Let's take a few moments to look at the numbers. A study conducted by the American Council of Life Insurers conclude that:

- 92% of financial planners say that long-term care risk applies equally to women and men

- 80% indicate that the risk applies equally to married couples and singles

- 75% indicate that the risk applies equally to people earning 30k a year and those 150k a year

- 75% say this risk applies equally to you and your parents

- The same study showed that only 4% of consumers have adequate LTHC coverage

- 58% of consumers say they cannot afford to pay for LTHC

The National Council on Aging conducted a study that revealed even more of the dark side of this impending crises:

- Only 28% of parents have talked about LTHC with their kids

- 93% of parents say they do not want their children to take care of them if it means the children have to use college savings that are set aside for the grandchildren

    - However, 50% of adult children say they would do this in order to help their parents, even if it jeopardizes their own kid's ability to attend college

- Anther 12% say they've already done so

- 90% of parents say they don't want their adult children to sacrifice there jobs

    - But 69% of adult children say they would do so. and of those who have already provided financial assistance, 57% say they used money they had set aside for their retirement, gotten a second job or raided a college savings fund

The average cost of LTHC is 45k annually according to ACLI. The average daily cost of caregiving for adult daycare is $50 and $121 for care provided in nursing homes.

According to the National Association of Caregivers, family caregivers give up an average of $659,139 in lost lifetime wages, pension benefits and Social Security earnings due to missed work from taking care of loved ones.

The National Center for Women and Aging conducted a survey that found:

- 67% left work early to provide care

- 64% used vacation or sick leave to provide care to a family member

- 69% arrived to work late or left early to provide care

- 29% gave up a promotion to continue to provide care

- 25% refused a job transfer due to caregiving obligations

- 22% took unpaid leave

- 20% cut work to part-time to provide care

- 16% quit their job to care for a relative

- 13% retired early

But wait, it gets worse. The Journal of American Medical Association found that 40% of care- giving spouses suffer from depression. According to the University of Pittsburgh Center for Social and Urban Research, individuals who begin to provide care for their husband or wife are 63% more likely to die within four years.

One reason so many people are ill-prepared to deal with the potentially devastating responsibility of LTHC is that most assume that this is something that will be covered by one of the following:

1. Health insurance
2. Medicare
3. Social Security

The truth of the matter is that neither of the above will cover the cost of LTHC. You can let Medicaid pick up the tab…if you are truly indigent. Hopefully, if you are reading this book, you won't ever come close to meeting the qualifications for indigent care… This would mean that you have little to no money. You would probably have to live in a government subsidized nursing home. The news reports are full of stories about the abuse and mal nourishment of the patients in those places. That's uncle Sams LTHC plan for you. With a little bit of forethought, you can come up with a better plan for yourself. In fact, if you are age 59 or younger, chances are that you can afford a LTHC policy. It doesn't start to become really expensive until you reach the age of 65 or above. Even beyond the age of 65, it's still more cost effective to purchase a LTHC policy than to pay out of pocket for long-term care.

It's unfortunate that one of the biggest looming crises to ever affect our society can very easily be circumvented if so many people didn't have the mentality that they are somehow exempt from being impacted by a LTHC situation. Let me share some more interesting stats from ACLI:

- By 2030 the over 85 population will be the fastest growing segment of the population
- By 2030 half of all women who reach 65 will reach 85; halfof all men will reach 82
- Amongst those age 65 who will require LTHC at some point:
    - Women: One in two
    - Men:One in three
- Nursing home population will reach more than 5 million residents by 2030

From the Center for Aging Research & Education:

- 75% of all nursing home residents are women
- 67% of elderly home health care recipients are women
- 73% of family caregivers are women

No matter your age or what your current retirement plan consist of, if it lacks a LTHC policy your plan is incomplete at best and leaves you and your family exposed to a potentially devastating turn of events should you or your spouse ever experience a long-term health crisis. Even if you already have sufficient resources to cover the costs of LTHC it still makes more sense to purchase a LTHC policy because your dollar for dollar savings in many cases would approach or exceed the 7-figure threshold. Besides, you probably planned to leave your money to your heirs in the event of your demise. There's no point in giving it all the medical establishment.

One last bit about insurance before we move on. I hope that it goes without saying that everyone should have adequate life insurance coverage. If you have not attended to the matter of protecting your family in the event of your death please don't delay in obtaining a policy asap. Even if your application for life insurance has been turned down due to such conditions as heart disease etc don't assume that you will also be turned down for LTHC insurance. The two are very different from an underwriting standpoint in that LTHC insurers don't care if you die. To them, your death means the end of the agreement, thus the end of their obligations. So, remember that one policy/application has nothing to do with the other. So even if your life insurance application was denied, please do yourself and your family a favor and obtain LTHC insurance.

CHAPTER 10

RETRACING OUR STEPS

"Believe you can and you're halfway there".~ Theodoore Roosevelt

I hope by now, you realize that this book was more about principles than anything else. My sensei, Grand Master Don Harbor used to always say, "If you understand the principles, the techniques will come naturally". He was so right. I would take long breaks from training due to injury and sometimes when I came back, I would have a hard time memorizing some of the jujitsu techniques. But it was the principles that never left me. Because I understood the principles behind the techniques it was never long before I just kind of naturally flow into position for the choke or the joint lock I was looking for. It's very much the same with the lessons in this book. I presented the case studies to you in story format in an effort to not only provide proper context but also to give you perspective so that I could illustrate the anatomy of a typical note deal in such a way that it might be easily relatable. I feel that it's important that the reader is able to relate to the characters so that you can see that these are average everyday Americans engaging in a form of investing that predates most all other forms of investing and commerce that exists today. I want you to see that anyone can do this. Regardless of whether you're permanently bound to a wheelchair, a professional athlete, a blue-collar worker or reality TV star. The same strategies that are employed to generate a 36% ROI on a $60,000 investment can be used to reap equal or greater returns on a $7,000,000 investment. If you were paying attention, you would notice that I gave you seven steps. I chose intentionally not to list them earlier in the book because I wanted you to read and learn. Everybody's looking for a quick fix. Well I'm sure you can tell by now that this aint a quick fix. On the contrary, this is about evaluating your life, determining what you want your life to look like going forward and establishing goals followed by specific actions designed to help you reach those goals. We can summarize all of that into this 7-step process:

7 Steps to Financial Freedom Outlined

1. **Evaluate your financial situation** – We saw in chapter three how Susan was presented with a potentially lucrative investment opportunity that pretty much forced her to sit down and reevaluate her life and her finances. Susan knew that she would be facing retirement in a few years and based onher current plan, her earnings just weren't enough to get her to where she wanted to be. So, she set out to do something about it. This was a pivotal moment in her life and had she not taken the time to look at where she was and where she wanted to be there's no doubt in my mind that she would end up like so many other Americans…stealing from the cat. This is the foundation of it all. This is something that you have to do as well. You have to take a good hard look at your life. Not just your finances but your entire life. Are you living the life that you chose, or are you living the life that just kind of happened while reacted to the world around you? Are you the architect of your lifestyle or did you just happen to come to occupy a life that someone else designed for you? This is an important thing to ponder.

There are so many important questions we can ask ourselves about this experience that we call life but the most important question to ask yourself is, "am I free?" Am I free to live life on my terms and if so, based on my future goals and the performance of my investment portfolio, am I on track to maintain that freedom perpetually? In order to accurately answer that question, you need to follow the next step…

2. **Assess your critical capital needs-** One of the most important aspects of freedom is financial independence. Financial independence means having enough money to:

   - **Cover your needs and basic wants**
   - **After taxes**
   - **After inflation**
   - **For some period of time (usually you and your beloved's lifetime)**

Susan also did an outstanding job of identifying how much money she needed to achieve financial independence…her critical capital needs. The amount of money necessary for financial independence is called "Critical Capital". This is a pile of money that can sustain all retirement expenses with inflation and after taxes for the requisite period. This may be an assortment of piles of money: note investments, real estate(brick and mortar), 401(k), IRA's, taxable money etc. If your investment portfolio doesn't meet your critical capital needs, you could find yourself stealing food from your cat during your golden years. I've included the formula for figuring your critical capital needs in Chapter two of this book. Take the time to figure out yours. Otherwise, you might wait too late and if you wait too late to plan you subject yourself to uncle Sam's plan…

3. **Identify suitable investments-** The next thing Susan did was identify suitable investments. In her case, there were at least two different forms of investment required to hit her target. She did a great job choosing and so can you. Here's where it can get tricky. There are so many options out there

in the market. Around every corner, there's a different guru claiming to have the holy grail of investment opportunities. Most of them are nothing more than slick salesmen looking to sell as many books, videos, and memberships as they can. They've figured out that 90% of the people listening to them will not take action no matter what. They also know that if they can just sell enough useless memberships, courses, and books that they don't ever have to worry about investing again. There are too many "gurus" peddling useless information. But they can get away with it because they set the barrier to entry so low that anybody can afford to buy. How many times have you seen an ad for access to some video training content that's like $37 and it's supposed to change your life? I chuckle every time I see one but in reality, it's getting way out of control. And at a time in history where there are probably more people looking for a safe haven for their investment capital it's becoming more and more of a challenge for them to figure out which way to go. My suggestion is to take your time and explore all of the options. Study the market as it relates to whatever investment opportunity you're considering and by all means, don't pull the trigger on impulse just because the guy in the video looks the part and talks a good game. Tune out the salesmen and let the numbers speak to you. Once you've chosen the right investment it's important to observe step four:

4. **Invest with fidelity-** I'm not talking about the brokerage house here. I'm referring to the level of commitment necessary to stay on track and accomplish the all-important goal of independence. This doesn't mean to stick your money into an investment and go bury your head hoping for the best. If you recall Sharon from Chapter 5 you'll remember that she epitomized investing with fidelity. Sharon had to sell part of a note at a discount, borrow money and pull off a few other maneuvers to raise capital

for a different investment opportunity. That's what I call staying ten toes down and sticking to the plan. Even if you choose to take a passive approach to investing, you should still watch your money. That means measuring the performance of your portfolio on a regular basis. I had a friend call me up recently seeking investment advice. She was interested in real estate investing. She expressed a fair amount of guilt around not having started sooner. She's now in her early 40's and she's starting to feel the encroachment of father time. When I asked if she was happy with the performance of her retirement account, she replied that her account is growing and that she felt that things should be ok by the time she was ready to retire. I asked her when was the last time she checked her earnings statement and she said she didn't remember. Just so happens she was sitting at her desk and had the statement right near her I encouraged her to not only take a look at the current statement but to also do a look back to see how her investments had performed the previous year. It didn't take her long to figure out that her portfolio had lost money last year. She was livid! As the conversation continued, I recommended that she go back and look at previous years. I understand that you judge the performance of stocks, mutual funds, etc over time just like many other investments. My point to her was simple, "if you don't know how your portfolio has performed historically and how it's performing now there is no way you can be sure that you'll have a shot at meeting your critical capital needs in this lifetime. You see, my friend took her eyes off the road. She just assumed that since she works for a big firm and the firm has a large brokerage managing their retirement accounts that of course, they must have things under control. She was mistaken. I explained to my friend that not keeping an eye on your portfolio and not knowing your critical capital needs is like having a flight scheduled to depart at 3 pm and leaving your house at 2 pm driving 40 mph with a 2-hour drive ahead of you. You may be going in the right direction, but you waited too late to leave and you're traveling at the wrong rate of speed. In my friend's case, she was anxious to start investing with me all of a sudden. But I refused to move forward with any investments with her until she had completed steps one and two and agreed to follow the rest of the seven steps. It didn't take her long to agree to that. She was mad about her retirement portfolio and understandably so. I've had similar experiences with many people over the years. Most people are ready for a change the minute they realize how far behind they are in terms of their earnings but still a lot of other people have unbreakable faith in their employer, stock broker or the system and just don't have the courage to separate from the herd. They're like cattle being led out to slaughter. Subconsciously they know what's coming but somehow the fact that they're not alone makes alright. The fact that you're still reading confirms that you are not a member of the herd. And for that I commend you. So, invest with fidelity…fidelity to your own personal plan for financial independence and nothing else…

5. **Resist the temptation prioritize form over function-** This one's huge for a lot of people. Philosopher, Umberto Eco once stated, "Nothing is more fleeting than external form, which withers and altars like the flowers of the field at the appearance of autumn". He hit the nail on the head. There's really not much more I can add to that. I'll just remind you of Jasmine from chapter seven. She lived a life that was a textbook example of form over function and it cost her almost $300,000. I imagine that it's costing some of the people I know a whole lot more than that. It's really not that important how much stuff you own if the sum total of all your assets is little to none. A homeless person with a net worth of zero might be better off than you if you own a home and have other liabilities that result in you having a negative net worth. Think about that the next time you see a guy in a luxury car give money to a homeless person... Big Willie might need to ask the homeless person to let him hold a couple bucks. I'm not at all against giving to the homeless – just making a point. If you're grounded and secure in who you are

you won't feel the need to squander your wealth for aesthetic appeal. If you have self-love, it's easy to play to win.

6. **Account for LTHC- the** previous chapter was all about LTHC. I kept it short and full of impactful information for a reason. I suggest you go back and read it again and share it with your loved ones. Please don't take this one lightly. I chose to place it towards the end of the book to make sure that it didn't get lost in the fray. So, whatever you do, don't underestimate the importance of this one. Many years ago I had to contend with this on a personal level and had I been a man of lesser means, this book might be entitled something totally different...

7. **Live Well-** With all the talk about money, investments and wealth I think it's important to remind you that the ultimate goal is to live a good life. That doesn't just involve accumulating assets just so you can pass them on to your heirs. You've gotta live! Whether that involves traveling, boating, building the business of your dreams or doing anything that inspires you to be better. If it brings joy to your heart you need to do it and do it often. If your whole life is nothing but work and sacrifice then you have to balance. It's perfectly ok to make seeking balance one of your main priorities in life. That one goal alone can add years to your life. And lastly, I just want to encourage you to give often. It doesn't have to be anything of monetary value but give something of value. If you do you will reap the reward that is inescapable. That's the reward of good karma. When you give with no expectation of receiving anything in return you will be rewarded with the great gift of universal reciprocation. Just like no debt in the universe goes unpaid, no good deed in the universe goes unreciprocated. Also, remember if some stranger randomly does a good deed for you and you know you'll probably never see him again, be sure to someone else to do a

good deed for – even if it's another stranger. That's called paying it forward. With all the stressors of life, work, and the pressures we place on ourselves to improve it's vitally important that we take the time to remember that it's not just about living. It's about thriving and being the best human being you can possibly aspire to while being gentle and patient with yourself and the world around you. This is my idea of living well. You may have your own. I hope you do and I hope that it inspires you to jump out of the bed and give life a high five every morning. And if you are fortunate enough to get out of bed in the morning remember to always let gratitude be to first emotion of the day. That's right, before the rest of the world can have any part of you it's important to give all of yourself over to the feeling of gratitude. Even if it seems like you don't have much, be grateful for what you have. If it's just a beat-up bottle of water, be grateful. One sip of water taken in a moment of sincere gratitude can mean more to you than winning an Oscar or Grammy, depending on the condition of your body in that moment. This is how I start my day. I suggest you do the same. I could have very easily and appropriately placed this at the very beginning of the book, but then if I had I would've lost many of you before I got into the really good stuff. So start with gratitude follow the steps and live well, my friend…

CONCLUSION

Well, you made it through to the end. We covered several strategies and each of them had multiple moving parts. You learned how to become the bank. You also learned how what might appear to be a disaster to the untrained eye can result in a good investment rapidly evolving into a great investment when a loan goes dark. We learned about partials and how powerful they can be in making up lost ground as well as how they represent a low barrier to entry for new investors with limited investment capital. We also took a look at a private money strategy for turning huge profits on short term loans (an ideal strategy for those seeking short term profits).

One thing that I did not cover in this book is sourcing the deals. If you have an interest in turning several of these transactions per year you either have to have a well put together marketing plan and budget or work closely with someone who does. I could write a book on the topic of marketing for deals as I have considerable expertise in this area. However, you don't need to be an expert – you just need an expertly crafted plan to locate and engage your target. This can be done via mail or on-line via a variety of platforms. One important point to be mindful of is that there are several note investment strategies that can be used to create wealth. Some of them we did not discuss in this book such as non-performing 2nd position liens and notes secured by commercial properties. These can be very lucrative niches to explore once you have gotten your feet wet with performing residential notes. But I wouldn't recommend them to someone just starting out in the business. Besides, there's plenty of money to be made in the performing residential note space. If you're going to do your own marketing you'll need to have a clearly defined target in terms of the type and location of the notes you're going after.

There are some companies out there who claim to provide note deals but in actuality what they do is locate picked over, undesirable notes for sell in some online repository or trading website and they bring you the note hoping to get a hefty commission for doing something you could do yourself. As for those online trading sights, I can't vouch for them as I've never had to use one but I have heard less than favorable reviews about some of them around the industry. Axiom provides fully vetted note deals to investors on our approved buyers list. Not only do we create notes that we sometimes offer for sale but I have created a system that gives us access to hundreds of millions of dollars' worth of real estate notes on a consistent basis. If you'd like to be considered for our approved buyers list, please call the office or email us at info@housemoneynation.com.

Whether you're flushed with cash or working with limited resources, seeking quick returns or looking for a long term play, there's a suitable investment strategy for you. You may even decide to do as I've done for years - invest in a mix of short and long term note deals. The best part about it is no-matter which strategy you choose, you can do it from wherever you are in the world. You don't have to break the normal rhythm of your life or quit your job. You can invest from the beach or anywhere else for that matter. I have friends all over the world who invest in notes here in the U.S. As the lender, you're listed on the home owner's insurance policy. So if the house burns to the ground you get paid off first. You have the power, control and protection.

Some readers will want to use this information to put together their own portfolio of real estate notes. Others will decide that they'd rather seek the aid of a professional to handle all the heavy lifting. If you're the former, starting out you should seek the assistance of professionals experienced in this industry. If you're of the latter, please visit www.axiomnote.com or call our office for assistance. Whichever route you choose, you and your family will be better for it.

ABOUT THE AUTHOR

With over 25 years of combined experience in residential and commercial real estate as well as note investing, Stan Steele brings a wealth of knowledge and value to every relationship. Stan was named one of the Top 100 People in Real Estate for 2019 by The Top 100 Magazine.

Stan is the founder and CEO of Axiom Note Trade, a professional note buying company that specializes in the purchase of seller-financed mortgage notes and trust deeds. As a real estate investor, Stan has renovated well over 200 properties and controls a portfolio that includes seller-financed notes, large tracts of undeveloped land as well as single-family homes and apartment buildings around the country.

As CEO, Stan is responsible for the overall vision of the company and oversees the marketing efforts as well as the acquisitions. Prior to his roles with Axiom, Stan spent 15 years as a successful mortgage banker. He is a certified mortgage planning specialist (CMPS) and has devoted the past 25 years to real estate investments.

Stan also shares his knowledge and uses his experience to guide and educate others in the industry through live networking events and his various meetup groups. He currently teaches a national real estate course approved by the National Association of Realtors (NAR) and he also offers courses for financial planners that are approved by the Certified Financial Planner (CFP) Board of Standards. These courses focus on strategies to help professionals protect and better position their clients for success through the utilization of advanced mortgage planning techniques that are designed to work in conjunction with wealth creation and taxation strategies for primary residence and income-producing properties.

Stan is also the host of "House Money Radio", a podcast dedicated to the education of note investors and real estate developers nationwide. He is the author of the book, "Big Money Secrets" – published in October of 2019. The book's core focus is building wealth through the utilization of seller-financed notes. You can connect with Stan at www.bigmoneysecrets.com

You can contact Stan at:
Axiom Note Trade LLC **www.axiomnote.com**
1775 Parker Rd. Building C - Suite 210 Conyers, GA 30094
stan@axiomnote.com Offc: 678-496-3427

Connect with Stan on Social Media

Stay in touch with Stan by visiting www.bigmoneysecrets.com

Subscribe to the "housemoneynation" YouTube Channel or Spotify to listen to HOUSEMONEY Radio podcast episodes. The Housemoneynation team is busy producing great and informative content to enrich your life! You can engage Stan there. He welcomes your honest feedback on this book and all of our content.

You can connect with Stan on Facebook at Mr.Eighthwonder, Linkedin.com at Stan M. Steele, CMPS Please give your honest feedback on this book

Stan is also the organizer of several meetup groups on meetup.com where he hosts and visits regular live meetups around the country. Connect on Meetup.com at Stan M. Steele, CMPS and be sure to join his "WHYFI" & "Seven Streamz" groups. Stan looks forward to connecting with you.

Wealth-building is not at all about get-rich-quick schemes. It's about identifying critical capital needs, planning, and investing with fidelity. It's not a sprint, it's a marathon.

"The Marathon Continues..."~ Nipsey The Great

REAL ESTATE VOCABULARY - DEFINITION OF WORDS AND TERMS

BIG MONEY SECRETS

REALESTATE VOCABULARY - DEFINITION OF WORDS AND TERMS

ACCELERATION: A clause in a mortgage instrument permitting demand for full payment of principal upon default.

ACKNOWLEDGEMENT: A formal declaration before an authorized (usually a notary public), by the person who executed a document, stating that he did in fact execute it. The notary public signs and puts his seal on a written statement describing the declaration. This written statement, or acknowledgement, is required on most instruments before they may be recorded.

ADD-ON INTEREST: A method used in installment lending. The interest rate is applied to the loan amount, then multiplied by the number of years of the loan term. The amount is divided by the number of months in the term to produce the monthly payment. This contrasts with the changing interest on the declining unpaid principal balance.

AD VALOREM TAX: Tax levied on property according to its value.

ADJUSTABLE INTEREST RATE: An interest rate that goes up or down as a certain designated monetary rate rises or falls.

ADJUSTABLE RATE MORTGAGE (ARM): A type of mortgage agreement that allows for periodic adjustment of the market. California law stipulates that a borrower can repay his loan without prepayment penalty if the variable rate should go up.

AFFIDAVIT: Latin for "has pledged his faith". A written

statement subscribed and sworn to, before a notary public, commissioner, consul, o administer oaths.

AGENT: One who acts for another. The latter is called the principal.

AGREEMENT: A meeting of the minds between two or more parties, which may or may not constitute a contract.

ALL-INCLUSIVE DEED OF TRUST {AIDT): Similar to a wrap-around mortgage; used when selling a property without paying off an existing deed of trust; this is a 2 nd position deed of trust that wraps around or "includes" the 1st deed of trust; the end-buyer makes payment to the seller on the AIDT, and then the seller uses the funds to make payment on his underlying 1st deed of trust. See WRAP-AROUND MORTGAGE.

ALTA TITLE INSURANCE POLICY: A type of title insurance issued to lenders that gives greater coverage than a standard policy by insuring against additional items, such as unrecorded physical easements, unrecorded mechanic's liens, water, and mineral rights, facts a physical survey would show, and rights of person in possession. Formerly call an ATA title insurance policy. ALTA is abbreviation for American Land Title Association, a trade association of title insurance companies.

AMENITIES: Satisfaction of enjoyable living to be derived from a home; conditions of agreeable living or arising from location or improvements.

AMORTIZATION: (1) The liquidation of a obligation in equal installments. (2) The recovery of a capital investment over a stated period of time.

AMORTIZED LOAN: A loan that is completely paid off, including interest and principal, by a series of regular or level payments that are equal or nearly equal.

AMORTIZED NOTE: A promissory note that is paid off in installments of equal size.

ANNUAL STATEMENT: In California, a statement required by statute to be given by the holder of a trust deed to the owner of the property within 60 days after the end of each year. It itemizes and accounts for the money received during the year just ended, including a break down of the principal and interest paid, as well as a breakdown of payments into or out of any impound account.

APPRAISAL: The practice of determining the appraised value of a property, usually based on comparable market sales or, in the case of an income-producing property, based on the amount of income the property can generate.

APPRAISED VALUE: An estimate of the fair market value of the property as of date, made by a appraiser who has followed standard appraising methods.

ARBITRAGE: The act of borrowing money at one rate and lending it out at a higher rate for

ASSIGNEE: The party to whom an assignment has been made.

ASSIGNMENT: The transfer of rights or a property interest to a third person, who can receive no greater rights than those possessed by the transferor.

ASSIGNMENT FOR THE BENEFIT OF CREDITORS:

The voluntary transfer by a debtor of some or all of his or her property to an assignee or trustee, who sells or liquidates the debtor's assets and tenders to the creditors (on a pro rata basis) payment in satisfaction of the debt.

ASSIGNOR: The party who makes an assignment.

ASSUMPTION AGREEMENT: A contract, by deed or other form, through which a buyer undertakes the obligation of an existing mortgage; generally requires the permission of the lender.

ASSUMPTION FEE: A lender's charge for changing over and processing new records for a new owner who is assuming an existing loan.

ATTORNEY-IN-FACT: An agent authorized to do certain acts under a power of attorney.

BALLOON PAYMENT: Any payment on an installment note that is larger than the smallest regular payment. Usually it is one payment at the end of the term; however, it can be periodic lump sum payments of principal during the course of the loan.

BASIS: The sum total of capital invested in a property during acquisition. This can be inclusive of renovation/construction

BENEFICIARY STATEMENT: A statement by the holder of a deed of trust stating the amount of the unpaid principal on the note and other information about the debt. The holder is required to have this statement upon payment of a small fee. Also called an offset statement or a bene statement.

BILL OF SALE: A written instrument that transfers title to personal property the same way a deed transfers title to real property.

BLANKET MORTGAGE OR BLANKET TRUST DEED: A mortgage or deed of trust covering more than one piece of property. For example, it may cover an entire subdivision and, in the case of a blanket trust deed, provide for a partial reconveyance of individual lots as they are sold, or in the case of a blanket mortgage, provide for a partial release of mortgage as they are sold.

BROKER: An intermediary between buyer and seller, or between lender and borrower, usually acting as agent for one or more parties, who arranges loans or sells property in return for a fee or commission.

CAPITALIZATION: Methods of estimating a property's value by considering net annual income as a percentage of a reasonable rate of return on an investment.

Net Annual Income/Rate of Return = Value of Property

CASH ON CASH RETURN: The difference between cash income and cash expenditures on income property related to the total cash invested (down payment plus closing costs, excluding pro-ration). This return is subject to deduction for income tax or increase for tax shelter

CERTIFICATE OF CLAIM (FHA): A contingent promise of the FHA to reimburse an insured mortgagee for certain costs incurred during foreclosure of an insured mortgage, provided the proceeds from the sale of the property acquired are to cover those costs.

CERTIFICATE OF DEPOSIT: A receipt for funds deposited for a stipulated time period in contrast to a passbook savings account. The is negotiable and can be sold; it is not redeemable before the maturity date. Typically issued in large denominations for limited time periods. Not the same as a savings

CERTIFICATE OF REASONABLE VALUE (CRV): The VA's
written appraisal of the value of a property.

CERTIFICATE OF SALE: A issued to the buyer at an execution sale of judicial foreclosure sale. The holder of the is entitled to a deed if the owner of the property does not redeem it within 1 year.

CHATTEL: An article of property that can be moved; personal property.

CHATTEL MORTGAGE: A mortgage of personal property. Under the Uniform Commercial Code, the chattel mortgage has

CLOSING: The consummation of a real estate transaction wherein certain rights of ownership arc transferred in exchange for monetary considcration and other agreed upon consideration. Also called a loan closing.

CLOSING COSTS: Payments by buyers and sellers for cxpenses associated with closing a deal and transferring ownership. May include fees for inspection, title insurance, escrow services, proration of property taxes and insurance, attorney's fees, etc. Synonymous with settlement costs.

CLOSING STATEMENT: A statement from an escrow agent to the parties involved that accounts for all funds received into and paid out of escrow.

CLOUD: An outstanding claim or encumbrance which, if valid, would affect or impair the owner's property title.

COLLATERAL: Property, real or personal, pledged as security to back up a promise; usually a promise to repay a debt.

COMMISSION: A fee charged by an agent for negotiating a real estate or loan transaction.

COMMUNITY PROPERTY: Property acquired by a husband and wife while married and not separated, except property acquired by gift, will, or inheritance and certain other items by statue. Any other property owned by a husband of wife is separate property.

COMP: Also known as a comparable property similar to subject property and used as a basis or comparison in a market data appraising method.

COMPOUND INTEREST: The method used for savings account interest and most mortgage notes. Requires at the end of each interest period (in this case, at the end of each month), the interest earned for that pay period is added on to the principal balance, and then interest for the following pay period is calculated on the new principal balance. Thus, interest is converted to principal.

CONDEMNATION: The taking of property for a public purpose on payment or just compensation. The power of the government and those authorized by the government to condemn property is called the power of eminent domain.

CONDITION: A provision in a contract stating that the

contract will not go into effect or that it will terminate upon the occurrence (or non- occurrence) of some future event. For example, a contract to buy a piece of real property may be conditioned upon the buyer's obtaining a loan. Often called a contingency.

CONDITIONAL LOAN COMMITMENT: See Loan Commitment.

CONDITIONAL SALE: An agreement granting title to property after all payments have been made.

CONDITIONAL SALE CONTRACT: A contract of sale in which the seller keeps title to the property until the purchase price is paid. Under the Uniform Commercial Code, the conditional sale contract covering personal property has been replaced by the security agreement

CONDOMINIUM: A form of ownership of real property. Consists of title to airspace and an undivided interest in common areas. Typically used for multiple occupancy housing, but may be applied to industrial and commercial property aswell.

CONSTRUCTION LOAN: Open-end mortgage loan, usually for a short-term to the actual construction of a building on a piece of real estate.

CONSTRUCTIVE NOTICE: Notice that is considered (construed) by law to be the equivalent of actual notice, such as the notice given by public records.

CONSUMER CREDIT PROTECTION ACT: A federal law that includes the Truth-in-Lending Law.

CONSUMER GOODS: Goods bought to be used primarily

for personal, family, or household purposes.

CONTINGENCY: A condition that must occur before a contract goes into effect. See also Condition.

CONTINGENT LIABILITY: The responsibility assumed by a third party who accepts liability for an obligation upon the failure of an initial obligor to perform as agreed.

CONTRACT: An agreement that establishes enforceable legal relationships between two or more parties.

CONTRACT FOR DEED: Also known as a land contract. Usually drawn between individuals, it is a contract by which the purchase price is paid in installments over a period of time during which the purchaser has possession of the property, but the seller retains title until the contract terms arecompleted.

CONTRACT PRICE: The amount the seller is to receive for property, including relief from mortgages and other liens.

CONVENTIONAL LOAN: A loan that does not have an FHA or VA guarantee. Typically used to refer to home mortgages. Both banks and savings and loan associations make conventional loans. The majority of home loans are the conventional type.

CONVEYANCE: A transfer of an interest in real property.

COOPERATIVE: A form of ownership used typically in multiple unit housing. The buyer of a unit purchases shares in the co-op and receives the right to occupy a unit. A form of joint ownership of real estate. An alternative to condominium.

CORPORATION: An arti person, created by law that has

certain powers and duties of a natural person.

COSIGNOR: A person who signs a note as an additional maker to help another maker secure a loan.

COVENANT: A promise in a contract, deed or written instrument.

COVENANT OF SEIZING: Clause in a mortgage which warrants that the mortgagor has title to the property and the authority to pledge the property as collateral.

CREATIVE FINANCING: A term applied to which involves the lender providing some type of seller-financing or equity participation to allow the buyer to purchase the property. See also Equity Participation.

CREDITLOAN: Mortgage issued strictly upon the strength of a borrower, without great regard for collateral.

CREDIT REPORT: Data on a prospective borrower with respect to income, employment, property, and bill-paying record. Usually include entries in the public record arising from legal actions such as foreclosures, bankruptcies, judgments, convictions, etc.

CREDIT UNION: A cooperative group organized as a savings institution and for making loans at a low rate of interest to its members.

DAMAGES: The money a person can or should recover because of the wrongful act of another.

DEBENTURE: Bond or security issued without any collateral pledge, but secured by the general assets of the issuer.

DEBT: An obligation to be repaid by a borrower to a lender.

DEBT FINANCING: The use of borrowed capital to the purchase of investment property.

DEBTOR: A person who owes a debt.

DEBT-TO-INCOME RATIO: Also called debt ratio. The relationship of the borrowers' monthly debt to their monthly income. When calculating the debt-to-income ratio, debt should include principal, interest, taxes and insurance on the borrower's home, as well as all monthly payments on credit cards and installment loans.

DEBT SERVICE: The sum of money needed each month of the year to amortize the loan or loans.

DECIMAL EQUIVALENT: The value of a fraction expressed in decimal form. For example,½ = .SO in decimal equivalent.

DEED: A written instrument by which real estate is transferred to another owner. The deed is signed, sealed, and delivered by the seller.

DEED-IN-lIEU: deed in lieu is a deed executed by a debtor in default to convey ownership/ equitable title directly to the mortgagee in to circumvent a foreclosure

DEED OF TRUST: A written instrument transferring bare legal title to real property to a trustee, for the purpose of providing security for an obligation such as a Promissory Note. Also called a trust deed.

DEFAULT: Non-performance of duty; failure to meet an obligation when due.

DEPRECIATION: A loss in value from any cause, such as age, wear, or functional or economic obsolescence. For tax purposes, either one of two types of depreciation may be claimed: straight line or age life methods, in which the same amount of depreciation is claimed every year over the life of the asset; or accelerated methods, which claim more depreciation in the earlier years of the asset and less during the later years.

DEVELOPMENT LOAN: Money loaned for the purpose of improving land by building of streets and utilities so as to make lots suitable for sale or use in construction.

DIRECT-REDUCTION MORTGAGE: A mortgage which directs that all payments on the principal have to be used for the reduction of the outstanding balance.

DISCOUNT: The amount that is subtracted from the face value of a loan in order to increase the effective yield.

DISCOUNTED CASH FLOW: A mathematical procedure for reducing future income and expenditures to present value by applying a discount factor such as the time value of money. Used in evaluating income property and in purchasing notes and mortgage or note and deeds of trust.

DISCOUNTED NOTE OR MORTGAGE: A note or mortgage that is sold for less than the amount that is currently owed on it. The purpose of discounting notes and mortgages is to increase the yield or rate or return to the investor to more than the amount of interest that is being charged on the note. If an investor is buying a note with a current balance owed of $8,000, bearing interest of 12%, the investor will receive a higher rate of return than 12% if he pays less than $8,000.

DISCOUNT INTEREST: Interest that is deducted from the principal amount of the loan in advance by the lender on the day of the loan, thereby increasing the lender's yield.

DISCOUNT POINTS: A fee charged by a lender when making an FHA or VA loan to offset the lower interest rate the lender will receive compared with conventional loan interest rates.

DISCOUNT RATE: The interest rate charged on money borrowed by banks from the FED.

DOWN PAYMENT: The difference between the purchase price and the total amount borrowed on the property. Also called owner's equity. Buyer may also have to pay closing costs in addition to the down payment.

DUE-ON-SALE CLAUSE: A clause in a note or deed of trust giving the holder the right to declare the entire debt due and payable if the owner sells or contracts to sell the property. Also called a due-on- alienation clause.

DWELLING UNIT: The living quarters of one household.

EARNEST MONEY: A portion of the down payment delivered to the seller or an escrow agent by the purchaser of real estate with his offer as evidence of good faith.

EASEMENT: An acquired right of use or enjoyment, falling short of actual ownership, which an owner or possessor of land may have in the land of another.

EFFECTIVE AGE: The number of years indicated by the condition of an improvement.

EFFECTIVE RATE: An interest rate, when applied once a year, which produces the same total interest earnings as when the nominal rate is applied more often and the interest is compounded. For example, interest at 7 ¾ percent compounded daily is equivalent to an effective rate of 8.06 percent.

EMINENT DOMAIN: The inherent right of a sovereign power to appropriate all or any part of private property within its borders for a necessary use, with or without the consent of the owner, by making reasonable payment to such owner.

ENCROACHMENT: Any physical intrusion upon the property right of another.

ENCUMBER: To place an encumbrance upon property.

ENCUMBRANCE: In a legal or technical sense, anything that limits or affects the ownership of property, such as a lien, mortgage easement, or restriction. In the daily language of real estate people, the term usually means a lien.

ENDORSEMENT: A signature place on the back of a note or check to transfer ownership. An endorsement in blank guarantees payment to later holders. An endorsement without recourse, or endorsement, does not guarantee payment to later holders.

ENDOWMENT FUND: Money or property given for the permanent use of an institution, person, or the like.

ENTITY: A form of business organization.

EQUAL CREDIT OPPORTUNITY ACT: Federal legislation designed to give women the same credit opportunities as men.

EQUITABLE TITLE: The ownership held by a buyer after he has contracted to buy property, but before legal title has been conveyed to him.

EQUITY: The interest or value that a property owner has in his property, over and above any liens against it.

EQUITY-BUILD: The amount by which a mortgage is reduced over time. If the market value of the property does not diminish, to the extent that a mortgage is reduced, the owner's equity increases or builds. The term equity build-up means the same.

EQUITY POSITION: The ownership of property; contrasted with lending funds as a mortgagee.

EQUITY OF REDEMPTION: The right of an owner to redeem his property after he has defaulted on a mortgage, typically after the foreclosure sale.

ESCALATION: The raising of some item, such as the interest rate or size of installment payments. The right to escalate the interest rate or size of payment may be given by contract to the lender under conditions.

ESCALATOR CLAUSE: A clause providing that an item will be adjusted upward or downward under certain conditions. For example, a note may provide that the interest rate goes up or down as the cost of living index rate rises or falls.

ESCROW: The deposit of items such as money, deed, and other instruments by contracting parties with a neutral party, called an escrow holder or escrow agent, to be held until all the terms and conditions of the escrow are Upon such the escrow is closed and the items are delivered to the respective parties entitled to them.

ESCROW ACCOUNT: A loan trust fund or impound account. May be a bank account in the name of the escrow agency used for holding escrowed funds.

ESCROW OFFICER: An employee of an escrow agent who has the responsibility of handling and closing escrows.

ESTOPPEL CERTIFICATE: Legal form signed by mortgagee or mortgagor that states the unpaid balance due on the loan as of a date and prevents, or "stops" any purchaser of the loan from claiming that the original borrower owes more than the stated amount.

EXECUTION: The act of signing by the involved parties of an instrument, usually witnessed or notarized for recording purposes.

EXPRESS: Stated in words, orally or in writing, as contrasted with implied, which is not stated in words.

EXTENSION AGREEMENT: An agreement giving additional time in which to pay money or perform some other obligation.

FACE VALUE: The balance owed on a note.

FAIR CREDIT REPORTING ACT: A federal law requiring that a credit reporting agency provide access to its report to anyone that the agency has reported on. Persons may make rebuttal statements and the credit agency is required to include the rebuttal with their report.

FAIR HOUSING: Federal and state fair housing laws prohibit unfair housing practices and to protect consumers

FANNY MAE: A popular name for Federal National Mortgage Association (FNMA).

FEASIBILITY STUDY: Analysis of a project to determine how successful it is likely to be.

FEDERAL DEPOSIT INSURANCE CORPORATION (FDIC): An independent federal government agency responsible to Congress, providing deposit insurance for all national banks and those state banks opting for coverage. Mandatory for members of the Federal Reserve System. Regulates interest rates on savings accounts held by nonmember insured banks. Supervises banking operations.

FEDERAL HOME LOAN BANK: A federal organization that provides a service similar to the Federal Reserve System for member savings and loan associations. Through it, they can get long and short term loans.

FEDERAL HOME LOAN MORTGAGE CORPORATION (FHLMC): A federal corporation that provides savings and loan associations with a secondary mortgage money market for FHA, VA, and conventional loans. Popularly known as Freddy MAC.

FEDERAL HOUSING ADMINISTRATION: The Federal

Housing Administration is currently a division of the Housing and Urban Development Department (HUD). Noted primarily for its mortgage

FEDERAL NATIONAL MORTGAGE ASSOCIATION (FNMA): A federal corporation that provides lenders with a secondary mortgage money market for FHA and VA loans. Popularly known as Fanny Mae.

FEDERAL RESERVE SYSTEM: The system consists of the Federal Reserve Board and 12 regional Federal Reserve Banks, together with the more than 6,100 commercial bank members. All national banks are required to belong; state chartered banks may elect to join.

FEE: The fullest estate a person may own in real property. It is the estate almost all owners hold. Also called fee simple.

FEE APPRAISER: Also known as a appraiser; one who is not.

FICTITIOUS DEED OF TRUST: A trust deed recorded by a trustee that does not cover an actual transaction. The trustee may then in later deeds of trust refer to the trust deed and incorporate its terms without repeating them in the part of the trust deed being recorded. This saves recording fees.

FIDUCIARY: A person in a position of trust and who represents another; known as the agent.

FINANCE CHARGE: The total dollar amount of all charges and interest that the lender will charge the borrower over the life of the loan. The Truth-in-Lending Law requires disclosure of this charge for most loans.

FINANCIAL INTERMEDIARY: A institution which acts as an intermediary between savers and borrowers.

FINANCING STATEMENT: An instrument with the county recorder or secretary of state giving notice of an outstanding security interest in personal property. Also called a UCC-1.

FINDER'S FEE: A fee agreed to be paid to one person, called a , who locates another person (such as a buyer, seller or lender) desired by the party promising to pay the fee. The fee is payable when the deal is consummated. In real estate transactions, the may introduce the parties, but he may not engage in negotiations unless he holds a real estate broker's or salesman's license.

FIRST MORTGAGE: A mortgage that has priority as a lien over all other mortgages.

FMV: acronym for Fair Market Value - describes how much any kind of property, including a house, is really worth. The IRS, which came up with the term, fair market value as the price the house would sell for on the open market ex: the appraised value

FOREBEARANCE: The refraining from doing something that a person has a legal right to do.

FORECLOSURE: The procedure of enforcing a lien by the sale of the property covered by the lien.

FORECLOSURE SALE: The sale of property in a foreclosure. Most often it is the sale of the property securing a debt after default in payment.

FORFEITURE: The loss of some right, estate, or interest in money or property because of a default.

FRACTIONAL RESERVE BANKING: is a system in which only a fraction of bank deposits are backed by actual cash on hand and available for withdrawal. This is done to theoretically expand the economy by freeing capital for lending.

FREE AND CLEAR: Free means a freehold estate, and in this expression it means a free title. Clear means there are no money encumbrances against the property.

FREEHOLD ESTATE: A legal estate in land, commonly referred to as estate of inheritance. The two most important freehold estates are the fee simple estate and the life estate.

FRB: See the Federal Reserve Board.

FRONT MONEY: Money put up at the beginning of a transaction. It may be also be the extension of credit at a very early stage of the development.

FRS: See The Federal Reserve Bank System.

FUTURE VALUE: The value of an investment at some future date in time.

GENERAL LIEN: A lien on all property of a debtor, both real and personal.

GINNIE MAE: The popular name for the Government National Mortgage Association; functions under HUD. Buys mortgages on property for low and moderate income borrowers granted by FHA and VA insured lenders. By the tandem plan technique, it buys low interest rate loans and sells them to FNMA and absorbs the cost difference. The subsidy is ultimately met by taxes.

GOVERNMENT NATIONAL MORTGAGE ASSOCIATION: See Ginnie Mae.

GRADUATED PAYMENT MORTGAGE: A type of mortgage agreement that provides for lower payments than a constant amortization rate in the early years and higher payment in the later years. Also referred to as a Flexiloan.

GRANT: (1) A transfer of real property. (2) The use of the word grant in the clause of a deed that conveys the property implies a warranty that the grantor has not previously conveyed or encumbered the property.

GRANTEE: A person to whom property is conveyed.

GRANTOR: A person conveying property.

GROSS INCOME: Total income before deducting expenses.

GROSS RATE INTEREST: Interest charged under a procedure in which the interest is added in advance to the principal and the installment loan payments are calculated on the total amount.

GUARANTEE: The act of pledging by a third party to assure payment.

GUARANTY: A pledge by a third party to assume the obligation of another.

HARD MONEY: (1) Cash loaned: contrasted with soft money

which means credit extended rather than cash. These expressions are often encountered in such a term as hard money trust deed. (2) Some people use this term to mean a high interest or short-amortizing loan.

HAZARD INSURANCE: Insurance against damage to property from

HOLDER: Any person in possession of a document, security, or instrument that is drawn, issued or indorsed to him or her.

HOLDER IN DUE COURSE: A person who takes a negotiable instrument such as a note or check, in good faith for value before it is past due and without notice of any defects when it was negotiated to him. Certain defenses that the maker could have claimed against the original payee, such as payment in full or in part, or certain types of fraud cannot be claimed against a holder in due course.

HOMESTEAD ESTATE: The rights of the head of a family or household in real estate, owned and occupied as a house, which are exempt from seizure by creditors.

HUD: Department of Housing and Urban Development; regulates FHA, **GNMA,** and PHA.

HYPOTHECATION: To pledge real estate as security without surrendering possession of the property.

IMPOUND ACCOUNT: A trust type account established by the lender for the accumulation of funds to meet taxes. FHA mortgage insurance premiums, and/or future insurance policy premiums are required to protect their security. Impounds are usually collected with the note payment. Also called trust account or loan trust fund account.

INCOME PROPERTY: Real estate capable of producing net revenue.

INCOME RATIO: The relationship of the borrowers' monthly income to the housing costs on the proposed home.

INFLATION: The term applied to increase in prices of goods and services occurring without an increase in quality or value at the same time. A higher price for exactly the same product when compared to the past is an price. Due to the interaction of many complex policies.

INDEMNIFICATION: Where allowed, the right to reimbursement for expenses, losses, or costs incurred.

INDORSEE: The person who receives an indorsed instrument.

INDORSEMENT: The signature of the indorser (usually on the back of an instrument) for the purpose of transferring an instrument and establishing the limits of his or her liability.

INDORSER: The person who indorses an instrument, usually for the purpose of transferring it to a third person.

INSOLVENCY: The inability to pay.

INSTALLMENT-LAND-SALES CONTRACT: See Land Contracts.

INSTALLMENT NOTE: An instrument (note) in which the principal (plus interest usually) is payable in partial payments (usually

INSTALLMENT SALE: An income tax related term whereby buyer pays less than 30 percent of contract price in the year of sale and continues to make payments to seller in subsequent years, thus allowing the seller to avoid having to pay tax on the entire capital gain in the year of sale. Payment on principal received subsequently is treated as capital gains; taxable portion determined by application of percentage of gain, which is gain divided by contract price.

INSTITUTIONAL LENDER: An institution that makes a substantial number of real estate loans, such as a bank, a savings and loan association, or an insurance company.

INSTRUMENT: A writing executed as the expression of some contract, act, or proceeding; for example a deed.

INSURANCE VALUE: The cost of replacing improvements.

INTEREST: (1) Legally, any charge a lender or creditor makes for the use, forbearance, or detention of money, no matter how the charge is labeled by the parties. (2) In daily usage, the percentage charged by the lender.

INTEREST RATE: The charge made for a loan of money or use of credit, expressed as a percentage of the principal.

INTERIM LOAN: A short term loan, usually made while a building is being constructed. After the building is it is usually replaced by a permanent loan called a take-out loan.

INTERMEDIARY: An institution that accumulates funds primarily from savers and lends them to borrowers. All banks and savings and loan associations are intermediaries.

INTERVAL OWNERSHIP: An interest in property related to a right to use the property for time periods; serves an ownership right. Typically used for vacation properties.

INVESTOR: As used for income-tax purposes, an investor is a person who holds property primarily for future appreciation in value.

INVESTMENT-TO-VALUE (ITV): The amount of capital invested in an asset expressed as a percentage of the value of the asset

INVOLUNTARY LIEN: A lien imposed on property without the consent to the owner, for example, real property taxes and judgment liens.

JOINT NOTES: A note in which there are two or more makers who share equal liability on it.

JOINT TENANCY: A form in which title to property is taken. Each entity named in a deed has an undivided interest in the property with all other joint tenants. Here the term tenant does not mean a renter but rather an owner. In some states, surviving joint tenants may automatically succeed to rights of a deceased joint tenant. Contrasts with tenants in common.

JOINT VENTURE: A business entity composed of two or more people joined together to conduct a single enterprise for a It is treated legally almost like a partnership, but differs from a partnership by having as its object a single venture instead of a continuing business.

JUDGMENT: A determination by a court of competent

jurisdiction of a matter presented to it. Most often a judgment is for a sum of money.

JUNIOR LIEN: An inferior or subordinate lien. For example, a rst trust deed.

LAND CONTRACT: A security device used in the sale of real property. The buyer contracts to pay the purchase price in installments. The seller contracts to deed the property to the buyer when the purchase price is paid in full. The seller keeps legal title until the purchase price is paid in full. Also called installment-land-salescontract.

LAND LOAN: Money loaned for the purchase of raw land.

LATE CHARGE: A charge added by a creditor under his note or contract when the debtor makes his payment late or after a certain date.

LEASE: A grant and contract that gives one party (the tenant) possession in consideration of payment of rent to the property owner (the landlord).

LEASE-BACK: A device for typically used for income property. A user may construct a property for its use and sell it to an investor who leases it back to the user. Usually illegal on residential transactions.

LEASEHOLD: Property held under a lease.

LEASEHOLD INTEREST: The right to use and occupy property granted by an owner or lessor to a tenant under a lease or rental agreement.

LEGAL DESCRIPTION: A description of real estate to allow a competent surveyor to locate the property on the ground.

LESSEE: A tenant under a lease.

LESSOR: A landlord under a lease.

LETTER FORM APPRAISAL REPORT: A letter that gives a brief description of the property, the type of value requested, the purpose of the appraisal, the date, the conclusion of value, and the signature of the appraiser.

LETTER OF INTENT: A letter in which a tenant gives a commitment to occupy a certain portion of the property under certain terms and conditions when the project is completed.

LEVEL PAYMENTS: Payments of equal size.

LEVERAGE: A method of investing or buying property in which funds to make the purchase are borrowed at a lower rate than the effective rate of income from the investment or property. The higher the proportion of the purchase price that is borrowed, the higher the leverage is said to be.

LIABILITIES: Debts or claims against assets.

LIEN: A charge against property for the performance of an obligation. The property can be sold to satisfy the secured obligation.

LIEN RELEASE: A written agreement by a lien holder releasing the debtor from further obligation.

LIEN THEORY: Borrowers retain legal rights in the property pledged to the lender, who has an equitable interest in the collateral.

LIMITATIONS: A period of time as by state statures within which certain acts are to be performed to render them valid.

LIMITED PARTNERSHIP: A special type of partnership with one or more general partners who manage the business and are responsible for its debts, and one or more limited partners who take no part in its management and are not responsible for its debts.

LIQUIDITY: (1) The ability of a party to pay bills and debts as they come due. (2) The ease and speed with which an investment can be converted into cash.

LOAN: A granting of the use of money in return for the payment of interest.

LOAN BROKER: See Mortgage Loan Broker.

LOAN COMMITMENT: A promise by a lender to make a loan. A commitment by the FHA is a promise to insure a loan on a particular property to a particular borrower. A conditional commitment by FHA is a promise to make a loan on a particular property for any borrower later found satisfactory. A standby commitment is a commitment by one lender guaranteeing another lender payment of a construction loan when it comes due.

LOAN COMMITTEE: A committee in a lending institution that reviews and either approves or disapproves loan application recommended by a loan.

LOAN CORRESPONDENT: An agent used by a distant

lender to help the lender make loans.

LOAN OFFICER: An employee of a lending institution who has the duty of making loans and helping with the loan process. His decisions, at least on larger loans, are usually subject to the approval of others in the organization.

LOAN ORIGINATOR: A primary lender; the entity from which a borrower obtains funds. A seller of mortgages in the secondary market.

LOAN PACKAGE: A group of documents prepared along with a loan application to give a prospective lender complete details about the proposed loan, property, borrower, and so on, and hopefully to persuade the lender to make the loan.

LOAN SHARKING: The deliberate charging or receiving of interest on monies in excess of that allowed by statutory law.

LOAN-TO-VALUE RATIO (LTV): The percentage of the value of a property that a lender can or will loan to a borrower.

LOAN VALUE: The appraised value of property when it is considered as security for loan purposes. This value is often lower than market value.

LOCK-IN CLAUSE: A clause in a note, mortgage, or trust deed setting a period during which no prepayment is allowed on the loan.

LOW-COST HOUSING: Housing designed to rent at low rates. Usually such housing is government aided.

MAI: A designation for a member of the American Institute of Appraisers, a part of the National Association of Realtors. The initials stand for Member of American Institute.

MAKER: The person who signs a note agreeing to pay it. Also called the payor.

MARGIN OF SECURITY: The difference between the amount of a loan secured by property and the appraised value of the property.

MARKET PRICE: The price paid regardless of motives, pressure, or intelligence.

MATURITY:

MECHANIC'S LIEN: A lien given by statute to persons supplying labor, materials, or services to improve real property. To perfect the lien, certain notices and recordings are required.

MOBILE HOME: A movable dwelling unit, built completely in a factory and designed as a permanent residence. It may be transported to a homesite by special equipment. It cannot be towed behind a car like a trailer.

MOBILE HOME MORTGAGE: Mortgage loan on a large mobile home considered to be a real property; usually drawn for a shorter period than a conventional real estate mortgage.

MORATORIUM: A temporary suspension of payments due under a agreement in order to help a distressed borrower recover and avoid a default and foreclosure.

MORTGAGE: A loan secured by an interest in real estate. A document which sets forth an agreement between a lender and a borrower and provides for a legal interest in real property to be held by the lender until the debt is extinguished. Property thus encumbered is called mortgaged. A promissory note is a contract to pay a debt, while a mortgage is the document that provides security for the promissory note. In the event of default on the promissory note, the mortgage allows the lender to foreclose and sell the property in order to recover the money that was lent. Deeds of trust are sometimes called mortgages, however, there are technical differences between the two contracts.

MORTAGE BACKED SECURITIES: Securities sold by Freddie Mac and others to generate funds for secondary market activities. Securities represent an interest in mortgages and, if sold by FHLMC, for example, they are guaranteed against loss of principal of interest.

MORTGAGE BROKER: who joins borrower and lender for a real estate loan, thereby earning a placement fee.

MORTGAGE COMPANY: A company that deals in real estate loans that are easily saleable in the secondary mortgage money market.

MORTGAGEE: The lender of money and the receiver of the security in the form of a mortgage, either by origination or assignment of the original mortgage.

MORTGAGE GUARANTY INSURANCE CORPORATION

(MGIC): A private corporation guaranteeing payment of mortgages and deeds of trust.

MORTGAGE LOAN DISCLOSURE STATEMENT: A statement in a form approved by the Real Estate Commissioner disclosing certain required information about a real estate loan. A mortgage loan broker must give this completed statement to the borrower before the borrower becomes obligated on the loan.

MORTGAGE MONEY MARKET: The source of for real estate. It is divided into two parts: the primary mortgage money market consists of all the sources of loans made directly to lenders; the secondary mortgage money market consists of all buyers of existing real estate loans and all the sources of using existing real estate loans as collateral.

MORTGAGE PORTFOLIO: The aggregate of mortgage loans held by the lender.

MORTGAGE RELEASE: A disclaimer of further liability on the mortgage note issued by the lender.

MORTGAGE RISK: The hazard of loss of principal and/or interest in the loaning of funds secured by a mortgage.

MORTGAGING OUT: Securing a loan upon completionof

MORTGAGOR: The borrower in a transaction where real property is used as security for the loan.

NATIONAL ASSOCIATION OF REALTORS {NAR): The national organization of real estate boards, a real estate trade organization. Formerly called the National Association of Real Estate Boards, abbreviated NAREB.

NATURAL PERSON: A living person, as contrasted to a

NEGOTIABLE INSTRUMENT: An instrument,

such as a check or note, that meets certain legal requirements that allow it to be transferred free of most claims the maker had against previous holders.

NET WORTH: An accounting computation of the value of a business; the owner's equity; stockholders' equity. The difference between assets and liabilities. The book value of a business or other entity.

NOMINAL INTEREST RATE: The rate of interest stated in a note or contract. This may not be the true or effective rate (actual cost) to the borrower.

NON-JUDICIAL FORECLOSURE: A foreclosure by having property sold to satisfy the debt without going through court process.

NOTE: An instrument in which one party, the maker or payer, promises to pay a sum of money to another, the payee, at a or determinate future time or on demand.

NOTICE OF DEFAULT: The formal notice that foreclosure proceedings have started on a piece of real estate due to the default on the note and mortgage.

NOTICE OFTRUSTEE'S SALE: A notice provided by law requiring the trustee to advertise the property in default, once a week for a period of 21 days, in a newspaper of general circulation.

NOTE TRADE: The act of trading, selling, assigning or otherwise transferring the interest in or rights to collect on a stream of payments

OBLIGEE: A person to whom a legal obligation or duty is owed; for example the payee of a note.

OBLIGOR: A person who has placed himself under a legal obligation; for example, the maker of a note.

OFFSET STATEMENT: A tenant's declaration of his interest in the property, sometimes called an estoppel statement. See also Statement.

OPEN-END CLAUSE: A clause that permits the outstanding balance of the loan to be increased by the borrower under the provisions outlined in the agreement.

OPEN-END DEED OF TRUST OR MORTGAGE: A trust deed or mortgage that secures not only that original debt but also future advances made after the date of the trust deed or mortgage.

OPTION: A contract that gives one party (the optionee) the right to enter some type of contract upon terms with another party (the option or). Usually the right given is the right to buy the optionor's property for a particular price.

ORIGINATION FEE: A charge by a lender for making a loan. Usually covers appraisal and credit report charges. May include the lender's payment to an independent or loan originator, which is therefore passed on to the borrower.

OWNER-FINANCE: Selling of real property on terms usually documented by a note and mortgage or note and trust-deed. In an owner transaction payments are made over a period of time. Otherwise known as Seller

PACKAGE DEED OF TRUST OR MORTGAGE: A trust

deed or mortgage secured by both real property and personal property.

PAPER: Any form of promissory note. Paper may be unsecured or it may be secured by real or personal property. Examples of paper include notes, mortgages, deeds of trust, contracts for deed, land contracts, etc.

PAR VALUE: The present value of an investment without any discount. Same as the face value or actual current balance owed.

PARTIALLY AMORTIZED: Loan repayment schedule that provides for equal payments of principal and interest up to a certain stop date, at which time the balance of the principal is due in full. See Balloon Payment.

PARTIAL RECONVEYANCE: A reconveyance that releases a part but not all of a tract from the lien of a trust deed.

PARTIAL RELEASE CLAUSE: A provision in a trust deed, mortgage, or land contract that permits the borrower or buyer to secure the release of part of the property by complying with certain terms, such as the payment of a certain sum of money.

PAYEE: A person to whom a note states it is payable.

PAYOR: A person who signs a note in agreement to pay it. Also called a maker.

PERMANENT LOAN: A mortgage loan granted for a long term based on the economic life of a property.

PERSONAL PROPERTY: Any property that is not real

property. Its outstanding characteristic is that it is movable. Also call chattel.

PHYSICAL PERILS: The cause of damage or destruction to example.

PLACEMENT FEE: Charge levied by a mortgage broker for joining a borrower and a lender who subsequently negotiate a loan agreement.

PLEDGE: Putting up property as security for an obligation by delivering possession of it to the creditor.

PLEDGEE: A person to whom a pledge is delivered.

PLEDGOR: A person who gives a pledge.

PMI: Abbreviation for Private Mortgage Insurance.

POINT: 1% of the principal amount of a loan. A lender often charges points when a loan is made, renewed, or assumed.

PORTABLE MORTGAGE: A mortgage which gives the borrower the ability to transfer his present mortgage at its current rate to his new house.

PORTFOLIO: A list of investments, trust deeds, and the like owned by an investor or lender.

POSSESSION: Occupancy: The highest form of "notice."

POWER OF ATTORNEY: An instrument authorizing a particular agent, called an attorney-in tact, to act for a principal.

POWER-OF-SALE CLAUSE: A clause in trust deed and in

some mortgages giving the trustee or mortgagee the right to sell the property that is security for the loan at public sale, without court procedure, if the debtor defaults.

PRELIMINARY TITLE INSURANCE REPORT: A report by a title insurance company showing the condition of the title to a property including liens, restrictions, and so on.

PREPAYMENT: To pay off all or part of a debt before it is due.

PREPAYMENT PENALTY: A charge provided in a note or deed of trust for the privilege of paying all or part of the debt before it is due.

PRESENT BALANCE: The amount still owed on a loan at a

PRESENT VALUE: The present discounted price or value of a single payment or a series of payment, taking into account the rate of return that an investor wants on his money.

PRIMARY LENDER: The entity from which a borrower obtains funds; a loan originator.

PRIME INTERST RATE: The best (lowest) interest rate given by banks to their most credit worthy corporate borrowers.

PRINCIPAL: A person who employs an agent.

PRINCIPAL PLUS INTEREST LOAN: A loan in which the periodic payments include a amount to be applied towards principal, plus interest on the unpaid principal amount of the loan.

PRINCIPAL RESIDENCE: The home in which the family

resides; the one used as the primary home and not for rental or investment purposes.

PRIVATE MORTGAGE INSURANCE (PMI): Insurance against loss available to mortgage lenders from private insurance companies.

PROMISSORY NOTE: A contract between a lender and a borrower used as evidence of the debt. May be secured by a mortgage or deed of trust.

PRORATION: The apportioning of expenses (such as taxes, insurance, interest and income; such a rent) between a buyer and seller according to the length of time such expenses and income had accrued or had been paid in advance

PURCHASE MONEY DEED OF TRUST OR MORTGAGE: A trust deed or mortgage given to secure all or part of the purchase price of real estate.

PYRAMIDING: Method of acquiring additional properties through

QUIET TITLE ACTION: A court action brought to establish title; to remove a cloud or defect on the title.

QUIT CLAIM DEED: A conveyance by which a grantor transfers whatever interest he may have in a property, without warranties or obligations.

REAL ESTATE: Also termed realty and real property; a portion of the earths surface extending downward to the center of the earth and upward into space, including all things permanently attached thereto by nature or man, and all legal rights therein.

REAL ESTATE INVESTMENT TRUST {REIT): A form of business organization authorized by the federal statute in which people may invest funds. The trust and investors get certain tax advantages. An equity trust invests in real estate. A mortgage trust invests in real estate mortgages and trust deeds. A combination trust invests in both.

REAL ESTATE MORTGAGE TRUST {REMT): The Real Estate Mortgage Trust; similar to REIT, but investment is made in mortgage securities, rather than real estate.

REAL PROPERTY: Land and things attached to the land, such as buildings, and other appurtenances.

REALTIST: A real estate broker holding active membership in a real estate board with the National Association of Real Estate Brokers.

REALTOR: A real estate broker holding active membership in a real Association of Realtors.

RECAPTURE: (1) Recovery of money invested in some investment. (2) A tax term describing depreciation allowances recovered at the time as asset is sold. At that time, accelerated depreciation in previous years claimed in excess of straight-line depreciation is treated as ordinary income instead of capital gain. The so treated is 100% of the excess minus 1% per month for each month the property was held over 100 months.

RECESSION: A state of the level of economic activity relative to a prior period. Measures used in judging the state include volume productive activity, such as Gross National Product and unemployment. Caused by interaction of complex economic forces, including reduction in which results in lowering of demand for goods and services.

RECONVEYANCE DEED: A deed from a trustee under a trust deed conveying legal title back to the property owner to release the lien of the trust deed. Also called a deed of reconveyance.

RECORDATION: The recording of an instrument in the county recorder'

REDEMPTION: (1) The correcting of a default under a trust deed or mortgage by paying up the amount past due. (2) The buying back or re-acquirement of property sold at a judicial foreclosure sale by paying the amount for which it was sold plus certain other items by statute. See also Equity of Redemption.

REDISCOUNT RATE: When a bank uses a customer's note as collateral for borrowing at the Federal Reserve Bank, the rate applied by the FRB is termed rediscount. The borrowing bank originally discounted the customer's note. Discount is interest charged inadvance.

REDLINING: The illegal practice of lender refusing to make loans in entire neighborhoods or areas thought to be declining in value.

REFINANCE: T f an existing loan.

REGULATION Z: Issued by the Federal Reserve Board to implement the provisions of the Truth-in-Lending Law (Consumer Credit Protection Act.). Not limited to real estate transactions. See Truth-in- Lending.

REINSTATEMENT: The curing of a default under a trust deed or mortgage by paying up the amount past due. Reinstatement restores the loan to the status it had before the default.

REIT: Abbreviation for a Real Estate Investment Trust.

RELEASE CLAUSE: A provision in a trust deed or mortgage allowing the owner of the property to secure the release of a part of the property upon certain terms, usually the payment of a certain sum of money.

RELEASE OFLIABILITY: A letter or other form release that relieves a debtor of any further responsibility on his debt or other obligation.

RELEASE OF MORTGAGE: A written instrument releasing the lien of a mortgage on real property.

RELEASE STATEMENT: A form prescribed by the Uniform Commercial Code to release all or part of a security interest.

REPLACEMENT COST: The cost of reproducing at current prices a structure having utility equivalent to the one being appraised.

REPLACEMENT COST COVERAGE: An insurance policy provision whereby full cost of repair is paid and do deduction is made for depreciation; owner receives new for old without contribution. Included automatically in all homeowners package insurance contracts.

REPLACEMENT VALUE: The cost to replace property

with comparable utility, quality, and features.

REQUEST FOR NOTICE OF DEFAULT: A notice a person may record requesting that he be if a notice of default is recorded under a particular trust deed.

REQUEST FOR RECONVEYANCE: An instrument executed by a trust deed holder directing the trustee to convey legal title to the property involved back to the owner. Most often a form for this request is printed on the back of the trust deed so that the creditor may execute instrument.

RESCIND: To cancel a contract or other transaction and restore to each party what he had given under it.

RECISSION: (1) The act of re scinding. (2) A legal action to rescind a contract or other transaction.

RESERVES: Portion of business earnings or bank assets set aside to cover possible losses, or withdrawals.

RESIDUAL: That which re mains; an appraisal technique to estimate the amount of net income attributed to the land, the building, or both.

RETURN ON INVESTMENT {ROI): See Capitalization.

REVERSE MORTGAGE: A type of mortgage which may be attractive to elderly householders because-it gives them regular cash income when they borrow against the value of their home.

REVERSIONARY CLAUSE: A restrictive provision in a deed to land that causes title to return to the granter if violated.

REVOCATION: The withdrawal of an offer or the cancellation of a right or license.

RISK ANALYSIS: A study made to determine the hazards and to evaluate their effects and repercussions.

ROLL-OVER MORTGAGE: A variation of the conventional and variable rate mortgage. A 30 year roll-over comes in six, 5-year segments. The roll-over mortgage is renewable every years, but at interest rates pegged to the then current cost of money.

RULE OF 78s: A method of computing payoff amounts for installments loans. Allows for greater earned interest for the early part of the loan term than if interest was charged proportionately.

SALE-BUYBACK: A technique in which a real property owner sells his property to a . At the same time he enters into a long-term installment contract to buy back the property. Usually illegal on residential transactions.

SALE-LEASEBACK: A transaction in which the owner sells his property and leases it back from the purchaser. Usually illegal on residential transactions.

SALES CONTRACT: A contract for the sale of property.

SALESPERSON: A person licensed to sell real estate and engage in other activities requiring a real estate license, but only as the employee of a licensed real estate broker.

SATISFACTION: Performance of the terms of a contract, usually by payment in full of an obligation.

SAVINGS CERTIFICATE: A time deposit account. Term is usually one year or more. Premature withdrawal is subject to interest penalties. Typically earns rates that are higher than passbook savings account rates are not considered negotiable, as is the ofdeposit. (CD).

SEASONED LOAN: A loan with a good payment record.

SECONDARY FINANCING: A loan secured by a junior deed of trust, especially a second deed of trust.

SECONDARY MARKET: The buying and selling of mortgages by lenders and investors; does not involve borrowers. Important government involvement through FNMA, GNMA, FHLMC.

SECURED LOAN: A loan subject to an agreement by the parties that in the event of default the lender has a legal right to the described property; entitles lender to have it sold and the proceeds applied tothe satisfaction of the debt.

SECURED PARTY:

SECURITIES: Stocks, bonds, and similar instruments evidencing ownership interest or debts.

SECURITY: Something given, deposited, or pledged to make secure the t of an obligation, usually the repayment of a debt; general mortgages, trust deeds, and other instruments backed by collateral pledges are termed securities for investment purposes.

SECURITY AGREEMENT: An instrument giving one party a security interest in the personal property of another as security for an obligation.

SECURITY DEPOSIT: A deposit put up by a tenant as security for f the lease.

SECURITY INTEREST: The interest of the secured party in personal property under a security agreement.

SELLER-FINANCE: SEE OWNER-FINANCE

SERVICING (LOAN SERVICING): The work of an agent, usually a mortgage company, comprising the collection of mortgage payments, securing of escrow funds, payment of property taxes and insurance from the escrowed funds, follow-up on delinquencies, and accounting for remitting principal and interest payments to the lender.

SERVICING FEE: Fee charges by mortgagee's local representative, who collects and inspects the property, and forecloses, if necessary.

SETBACK: The distance from a lot line which by law, regulation, or restriction in the deed must be left open; the linear distance between the lot line and the buildings or building line.

SET-OFF: A claim a debtor is entitled to make against a creditor that reduces or eliminates the amount the debtor owes the creditor.

SETTLEMENT COSTS: Charges associated with obtaining a mortgage loan. Included are title search and insurance, escrow, appraisal, credit report and attorney fees, and charge for real estate broker's services. Prescribed by the 1974 Real Estate Settlement Procedures Act. Does not set amounts, but requires prior disclosure on authorized form and distribution of HUD booklet.

Same as closing costs.

SETTLEMENT PROCEDURES ACT OF 1974: A federal law prescribing that lenders must provide borrowers with cost data in a form authorized by HUD at least one day in advance of the close of an escrow involving real estate. It does not regulate the amount of costs, only the advance disclosure of how much they are. See Closing Costs.

SOFT PAPER: Paper with very lenient terms, such as a low interest rate or long term amortization. The opposite of hard paper.

SUBORDINATION: The act of making an existing loan or leasehold secondary or junior to another lien or loan.

SUBROGATION: The substitution of one person in the place of another with reference to a lawful claim or right.

SUBSTITUTION OF COLLATERAL: A clause which allows a borrower to "move" the lien to another property by substituting another property as collateral for the loan.

SUBSTITUTION OF MORTGAGOR: An agreement in which the lender on a loan being assumed by a buyer agrees to relieve the original borrower of liability.

SUBSTITUTION OFTRUSTEE: An instrument that the b under a trust deed executes and records to substitute a new trustee for an earlier one.

SUPPLY AND DEMAND: The concept that that price or value varies directly but not necessarily proportionately with demand, and inversely but not necessarily proportionately with supply.

SURETY: A person who guarantees performance of an obligation.

SURVEY: The measurement and description of land by a registered surveyor.

SWEAT EQUITY: An ownership interest in property earned by the performance of manual labor on that property.

SYNDICATE: An association of persons who pool resources to invest in real estate.

TAKE-OUT LOAN: A permanent, long-term loan that takes the place of short-term construction loan.

TAX BRACKET: Refers to the printed tax rate schedules for both federal and state income taxes. Individual rates on the federal tax rate schedule start at 14% on the $500 of taxable income and go up to 70% on income in excess of $100,000.

TAX FREE EXCHANGE: An income tax related term; more properly called a tax-deferred exchange. An owner who trades a property for another of like kind may defer payment of income tax on a gain which would otherwise be realized by disposing of the property.

TAX SHELTER: An investment for which there is an operating loss due primarily to charging non-cash expenses such as depreciation. When this loss is added to the investor's other taxable income, his total income tax is reduced; hence his income has been "sheltered" from income tax.

TENANTS-IN-COMMON: A form of ownership of real

estate in which each tenant has an interest and can convey such interest independently of the others. Contrasts with joint tenancy. Used typically by persons not married to each other.

TERM: (1) A provision of a loan contract. (2) The length of time a loan, lease, or some other obligation or contract is to run.

TERMINATION STATEMENT: A statement from a creditor showing that a security agreement has been It should be where the

.

TERM LOAN: Non-amortized loan for a period, at which time the entire principal amount is due.

TERM MORTGAGE: One having a term, usually not over a year maturity, during which interest is paid but the principal is not reduced.

THIRD-PARTY JUNIOR FINANCING: A type of in which a third party makes a loan on existing property and agrees to take back a second, third, or even fourth mortgage deed of trust secured by a promissory note.

TIGHT MONEY MARKET: A period of time in which funds for loans are scarce, loans are hard to get, and interest rates and points charged by lenders are high.

TITLE INSURANCE: Insurance that insures the status or the title to a piece of property. A promise to indemnify up to the policy limit and subject to its terms, the insured owner, lender, or other interest for any loss suffered because of defect in or cloud on the title report and policy. Offered only by title insurance companies operating in the private sector.

TOWNHOUSE: An architectural term used to describe a type of housing; units typically having a common wall. Owner has title to the real property, unlike a condominium.

TRUST ACCOUNT: (1) An account into which a person places funds he holds in trust. (2) A special account in which a broker keeps funds he is holding for others. See also Impound Account.

TRUSTEE: A person who holds title to real or personal property for the A trustee is one of the parties in a trust deed.

TRUST DEED: Also called a deed of trust. Provides security for a trust deed note. The note is the evidence of the debt and the trust deed secures the loan or debt with the property. It acts similar to a mortgage, with the primary difference being in the way the title is held and in the manner of foreclosure.

TRUSTEE'S DEED: A deed given by a trustee under a deed of trust to the buyer of property at a trustee's sale.

TRUSTEE'S SALE: A foreclosure sale conducted by a trustee under a trust deed after a default.

TRUSTOR: A person who conveys property to a trustee. In a trust deed, the truster is the borrower or debtor.

TRUTH-IN-LENDING: A federal law requiring that the cost of credit be disclosed in a prescribed manner. The interest cost or charge must be expressed in terms of an annual percentage rate called the APR.

UNDERLYING LIEN: Underlying lien is a claim that has priority over claims of other creditors. Therefore it is repayable before the subsequent obligations are fully paid. For example, a mortgage has priority over second and third mortgages. Subsequent mortgages will be paid after earlier underlying liens have been paid.

UNDERWRITING PRINCPLES: The principles that determine the risks to lender and investor.

UNLAWFUL DETAINER ACTION: A fast legal action to recover possession of real property. Usually it is used by a landlord against a tenant, but it may also be used by the buyer at a trustee's sale against the former owner who refuses to vacate.

UNSECURED: Without security.

USURY: The charging of more interest that is allowed by law.

UTILITY: Usefulness; the ability to give satisfaction and/or excite desire for possession.

VALID: Legally effective.

VA LOAN: A loan guaranteed by the Veterans Administration.

VENDEE: Abuyer. **VENDOR: A** seller.

VESTING OF TITLE: The taking of legal title to property.

VETERANS ADMINISTRATION {VA): Veterans Ad ministration; since 1944, the VA has guaranteed the top portion of an eligible veterans loan.

VOID: {1) having no legal effect; null. {2) To have an instrument or transaction declared void.

VOLUNTARY LIEN: A lien intentionally put on property by

the owner.

WAIVE: To give up; for example, to waive a right.

WAIVER: The giving up of a right.

WARRANT: A guarantee

WARRANTY: A guarantee or undertaking that certain defects do not exist.

WASTE: Willful damage to property.

WHOLE LOAN: A term used in the secondary market to indicate that the full amount of a loan is available for sale with no portion, or participation, retained by the seller.

WRAP-AROUND MORTGAGE, TRUST DEED, OR CONTRACT FOR SALE: {Also called a "wrap.") A mortgage, trust deed, or land contract that includes a prior loan, called the underlying loan. It works like this: A debtor owns or buys property with a mortgage on it. Without paying off mortgage, the debtor sells the property, creating a mortgage, deed of trust, or land contract for an amount that includes the amount due on the mortgage. The new owner makes one monthly payment to the original debtor, out of which the original debtor makes the payment on the mortgage, keeping the difference for himself or herself. For example, John owns a house with a $60,000 mortgage. He sells the house to Tom for $80,000 without paying off the mortgage. Tom makes payments to John on the $80,000, out of which John then makes payments on the original $60,000 mortgage. The difference between the $60,000 and the $80,000 is called "the equity in the wrap."

YIELD: Interest earned by the lender on the money loaned. Also called rate of return. Yield is particularly relative to discounted paper. If paper is bought at a discount, the investor receives his yield from a combination of the interest that is being paid on the paper, as well as

ZONING: A legislative process by which restrictions are placed upon the use to which property may be put.